Emergent Curriculum

in Early Childhood Settings

Emergent Curriculum

in Early Childhood Settings

From Theory to Practice

Susan Stacey

Redleaf Press®
www.redleafpress.org
800-423-8309

Published by Redleaf Press
10 Yorkton Court
St. Paul, MN 55117
www.redleafpress.org

First edition 2009
Cover design by Soulo Communications
Cover photography by Bob Pearl
Interior typeset in Adobe Garamond Pro and designed by Soulo Communications
Interior photos and illustrations courtesy of the author
Printed in the United States of America
17 16 15 14 13 12 11 10   3 4 5 6 7 8 9 10

Wien, C. A., and S. Kirby-Smith. 1998. Untiming the Curriculum: A Case Study of Removing Clocks from the Program. *Young Children* 53 (5): 8–13. Reprinted with permission from the National Association for the Education of Young Children. Copyright © 1998 NAEYC.

Wien, C. A., S. Stacey, B.-L. H. Keating, J. D. Rowlings, and H. Cameron. 2002. The Doll Project: Handmade Dolls as a Framework for Emergent Curriculum. *Young Children* 57 (1): 33–38. Reprinted with permission from the National Association for the Education of Young Children. Copyright © 2002 NAEYC.

Library of Congress Cataloging-in-Publication Data

Stacey, Susan.
Emergent curriculum in early childhood settings : from theory to practice / Susan Stacey.
    p. cm.
Includes bibliographical references.
ISBN 978-1-933653-41-9 (alk. paper)
1. Early childhood education--Curricula. 2. Reflective teaching. I. Title.
LB1139.4.S73 2009
372.19--dc22
                    2008008879

Printed on 100 percent postconsumer waste paper

For my children, Michael, Jennifer, and Matthew,
who taught me about childhood,
and my devoted parents, Dorothy and Lewis,
who find joy in being in the company of children

Emergent Curriculum
in Early Childhood Settings

Foreword

As a child—or as a teacher—have you ever been bored in school?

For many of us, school was a same-old, same-old experience—a daily routine to be gotten through. True, as children we did learn the things that grown-ups thought were important for us to know. But the classroom wasn't often a place for learning about ourselves, our friends, or what really interested us in the world. That was more likely to happen at recess, in our neighborhoods, and at home—places where there was space and time to make choices, and friends to negotiate problems and enjoy solutions with.

As a teacher and caregiver of young children, are you ever bored? Life with the children can be pretty routine. Is your job just a schedule to be tolerated each day—for you, and perhaps even for the children?

Many children now experience child care from infancy on. For some of them, child care may be simply an earlier beginning of "school"—of doing what you're told, in a group. But that's not how young children and teachers learn best. In a well-ordered environment, young children are highly active, fascinated explorers of a world so new.

The children choose what to do, do it with great energy, and move on to the next challenge. The caregiver, watching the children, is an active learner too. She's asking herself: Who are these children? What do they care about? What are their skills? What are they practicing? What should I offer them next?

Teaching, at its best, is a creative act. Susan Stacey has written *Emergent Curriculum* to remind us of that fact. She offers, through real-life stories from her own experiences and from those of her colleagues, a framework for practicing the art of emergent curriculum.

There are two basic approaches to curriculum planning and development: preplanned and emergent. The lure of preplanned curriculum is strong; it's so easy to follow the directions somebody else has made up. And maybe you've been handed a fat book of activities and learning goals and told by your supervisor, "This is our curriculum." Maybe you've been told your lesson plans need to be written down and turned in ahead of time, so the center can demonstrate it's doing its job.

Young children know better. They don't learn just because we teach them. They learn when their interest is caught. They may not pay attention to your lesson if something else, in their heads and bodies or in the environment, is more interesting. Their bodies demand action; the world calls out for exploration. Children are wired to construct their knowledge of the world through constant practice.

If we want a world peopled by intelligent children and adults, we need to respond to children's inherent motivation to learn, which is at its height in early childhood. Teachers and caregivers of young children are at their best when they follow the children as models for their own adult curiosity, learning with them and about them. We watch the children, we think, we respond, and that's how curriculum emerges.

You can't write an emergent curriculum and package it for sale. Emergent curriculum is invented by its participants, which is more work for teachers and caregivers, because it requires continual alertness. It's also more fun and more educational, because it's full of surprises and new challenges. It can't really be written until after it's happened; emergent curriculum is *ex post facto* curriculum, which can be a problem for you if you're required to produce lesson plans in advance. In this book Susan Stacey deals helpfully with this dilemma, especially in a detailed look at the process of *documentation*, in which teachers take notes, pictures, and examples of children's work to create visual representations of children's emergent learning.

Many of the books college students and on-the-job teachers are asked to read are full of principles and best practices and theories and lists and lesson plans and study questions. They demand: "Are you learning what we're teaching you?" "Memorize it; it will be on the test." "If you're a good teacher, you will do it in your classroom." Strangely enough—or perhaps not so strangely—many early childhood practitioners *don't* do it in their classrooms (even though they passed the test).

As a college instructor in early childhood education, I frequently find myself in conversation with colleagues at other colleges, and their repeated lament is "How can we get them to do what we've taught them?" My response is that mostly, we can't. Teachers and other grown-ups, I've noticed, don't change their behaviors just because they've learned the principles of why they should adopt developmentally appropriate practice or any other theoretical model. We go through the effort of changing our behaviors if we're anxious about getting in trouble, if we're bored and looking for something new to try, or if we're inspired by a life-changing experience—which could take the form of stories about someone else's work with children.

Emergent Curriculum is a collection of stories about someone else's work with young children. Enjoy them—and as you do, ponder some of the explanations of *why* the teachers and caregivers worked with the children in these ways. If you were to try something similar, what would happen? Would your children run wild? Would you get in trouble for changing the lesson plan? Would you have new stories about the children to share with their parents? Would you learn new things about the world, about children, and about yourself?

Reading the manuscript of this book in preparation for writing this foreword was an interesting challenge for me. Every time I thought of something I could say and made a note of it, I'd read a little further and discover Susan had already said it. She really knows this stuff. And she hangs out with others who are working on it, too, and she's shared many of their stories in this book, as well as her own. We are not all alike; different voices are needed to create dialogue.

I got to visit Susan's program in New Hampshire and to see firsthand some of the stories she shares in this book. She was really doing it. So can you.

Elizabeth Jones
Pacific Oaks College

Acknowledgments

Early childhood educators need mentors—to cheer them on in their professional work and to help them remember the joys and inspirations in our field. I've been fortunate to have several: Carol Anne Wien, who continues to stimulate my thinking, Hilary Marentette, who many years ago encouraged me to follow my heart, and Elizabeth (Betty) Jones, who introduced me to Pacific Oaks College and has followed my career with joy, steady support, and a flow of thought-provoking questions that keep me in a welcome state of disequilibrium.

We also need colleagues with whom we can think, question, argue, and problem solve. Liz Hicks has filled this role for many years, as have Margie Carter and Deb Curtis, John Nimmo, Susan Hagner, Barb Bigelow, Gretchen Reynolds, Liz Rogers, and Teresa Cosgrove. Over the years, conversations with these thinkers have contributed hugely to my professional growth and have helped me keep passion in my work.

Many early childhood educators have shared their teaching in this book. This in itself is an act of generosity, for they have taken the risk of sharing their work, their struggles, and their successes with a wider audience. For me, they've taken the time to reflect, to engage in correspondence, to dig out and send hard-to-find files and photos. In short, they have been willing to do whatever it took to help bring this book to completion. Those educators are Bonnie Morin, Lori Warner, Katie Lugg, Carrie Dupell and Karen Felch at the New Hampshire Technical Institute Child and Family Development Center in Concord, New Hampshire; Susan Hagner and her staff at Emerson Preschool, also in Concord; the teaching staff at Jubilee Road Children's Center in Halifax, Nova Scotia; and the teachers at the Peter Green Hall Children's Center, also in Halifax, including Elizabeth Conrad, who bravely participated in the case study of removing clocks from the classroom when she was a member of my staff some years ago. Likewise, the early childhood students at New Hampshire Technical Institute have given me the opportunity to think through what does and what doesn't work for teachers in the classroom. Engaging in discussion with them, and with all the students I've worked with in both the United States and Canada, enabled me to articulate my thinking about emergent curriculum. I thank them all, whether students or seasoned professionals, both for their continuing openness toward generating curriculum with and for young children, and for their dedication to our field.

My editor, Beth Wallace, guided me through the process of creating a book and did so with admirable patience and good humor. She walked me through technical glitches, rewrites, and confusion. Beth knows about early childhood, and her work shows in this finished product.

I am thankful to the children whose work appears in this book. They continue to fill me with wonder for their insights and to astonish me with their capabilities. Finally, thank you to Brian, who hasn't seen much of me this past year as I worked through evenings and weekends. The laptop was a huge gift, but an even bigger one was his constant support for and pride in what I do.

Introduction
and Invitations

This book is an invitation for you to think deeply about curriculum for young children. Doing so is crucial, because the early childhood curriculum you provide has a profound and long-term effect on how children learn and, just as important, on how much they enjoy the process.

Perhaps you're an experienced early childhood educator who has heard and thought about emergent curriculum but you haven't yet had the opportunity to explore it in the classroom. Or you've studied the theories surrounding emergent curriculum and are wondering how to translate theory into practice. Maybe you are new to early childhood education and are wondering how to start the process of generating curriculum. Or you are required to follow a prescribed curriculum and wonder how to include more child-centered practices. Whatever your circumstances, you will have the opportunity throughout this book to reflect on what you believe about curriculum, what you want in your classroom, and what alternative choices there may be.

Your own values and beliefs—blended with your training and experiences and then translated into classroom practice—directly affect children's love of learning, their problem solving, and their engagement with materials, investigations, and people. We early childhood professionals have a tremendous responsibility to provide the best possible environments and experiences for children to construct both knowledge and relationships. And doing so takes careful thought, a willingness to explore and practice, and ongoing dialogue with other professionals.

Of course, your own education, experiences, and professional training also affect how you think about and generate curriculum. There are many choices to make. We teachers are surrounded by information from journals, workshops, professional development seminars, in-service training, and our own reading. We work with all ages from infants to school-age children, in half- or full-day programs, in homes or centers or public schools, in commercial or nonprofit settings—all with differing levels of autonomy and therefore with different opportunities for decision making.

Regardless of the setting, however, what is central to quality early childhood education is play. Self-chosen and directed by the child, it provides ample opportunities for learning. When children explore through play their own theories about how the world works, they become deeply engaged. Montessori teaches us that children learn best about that which they are interested in, and Dewey reminds us that children love to be engaged in real work; that is, they find out about the world by being in it, by constructing their knowledge through community projects that are meaningful to them. And Vygotsky teaches us much about social learning, between the children themselves and between the child and the teacher in the role of facilitator. This role is important, since teachers who value children's ideas want to support those ideas and take the children's learning to higher levels without interfering in their play—a delicate balance.

Children, of course, need no extrinsic motivation to play. In an interesting environment, they can play happily for hours. (Notice that I use the word "interesting" rather than "richly provisioned." Given the opportunity and extended time, children will engage in complex play using such materials as cardboard boxes, rocks, and sand.) In your own experiences, you may have seen play-based curriculum in action, or, on the other hand, observed play, being treated as something quite separate from curriculum. In my experience, when play is treated as separate from curriculum, it is limited to brief time periods, watched over for safety rather than for interesting occurrences, and, rather than becoming an opportunity for teacher reflection, is seen as an interruption in the "real" curriculum.

Perhaps play seems to be undervalued or forgotten because of the general erosion of childhood. When you think back to your own childhood, what do you remember playing at or with? How much time was there for daydreaming, relaxing, playing with found materials, being outdoors, inventing games with other children, and just "messing around"? My guess is that compared with today's child, you had more opportunity for those kinds of pastimes. Today's child is likely to live in a much more regimented environment, with play that is scheduled, after-school activities that require enrollment, car pools, and regular attendance, and much time spent in front of a computer monitor or a TV screen. In fact, it sometimes seems as if children do not know how to play in unstructured settings with an array of natural materials and lots of time. In such an environment, they are often at a loss.

When curriculum in early childhood settings comes from books of prescribed activities, or when teaching methods are held over from previous teachers and remain unexamined, curriculum becomes stale. Such a situation serves neither the children, who want and deserve interesting things to do and explore in order to construct knowledge, nor their teachers. Limited to a repetitive, mundane curriculum, a teacher finds it almost impossible to maintain energy and enthusiasm—much less passion—for her work. Rather than being something to look forward to, the teaching day becomes something to get through.

Sometimes teachers are required by a higher authority to teach in a particular way and feel they have no power to challenge that authority or to make changes. Other teachers, thrust into the practical demands of the field, feel overwhelmed or simply have no time to reflect on what they are doing. The children in their classrooms are safe and appear to be happy. Unless these teachers are provided with an alternative approach, they may feel this is enough. In such circumstances, we have to remember the potential of the child. In their early years, children are full of wonder and curiosity, as well as interesting ideas and theories. They are also extremely competent, an ability that is sometimes underestimated. For a young child, the day is full of possibilities to learn through play—to explore how a pulley works while acting out a construction site, to interact with print and money while playing restaurant, to problem solve while helping a disabled friend get onto a platform outside, or to develop fine-motor skills through combining playdough with scissors. It is a privilege to have the opportunity to harness children's willingness to investigate and to tap into their inborn curiosity to create a love of learning through interesting curriculum.

However willing a teacher may be to try interesting approaches that benefit children, other obstacles can get in the way of generating meaningful emergent curriculum. For instance, many educators are expected (by their supervisors as well as local or national authorities) to prepare curriculum well in advance. After all, teachers are accountable to those authorities as well as to families. How do teachers prepare somewhat in advance while also remaining open to the possibilities of what might occur day by day as children explore, discover, negotiate, and create worlds of their own through their play? How do teachers show in their curriculum development that they value the child and the child's ideas?

Now add to this puzzle the plethora of standards that have developed over the past twenty years—standards that guide teachers in developmentally appropriate practices, help them define and strive for quality care and education, and set guidelines for quality pre-service teacher education—and the dream of attaining a truly child-centered curriculum becomes more complex. All over North America and around the world, early childhood educators are more and more frequently required to link their programs to learning standards set by government departments or school boards. Whatever the reasoning behind these standards, and no matter how individual teachers feel about them, it is critical to value and protect learning through play in child-centered programs, while at the same time keeping the required standards in mind. If we in the teaching profession neglect these basic values about play or fail to articulate these values clearly and often to policy makers, we risk losing play as a vehicle for learning. In its place we may find ourselves surrounded by ever-increasing requirements that are not age or stage appropriate, and that fail to address the child's need to construct knowledge through hands-on, thought-provoking experiences.

An Invitation to Dream

Dream for a moment about being in a position of complete freedom in terms of what kind of curriculum you can provide for the young children in your care. You have access to research, to models of promising practices and awe-inspiring physical settings, to good-quality literature and professional development. And since you're dreaming, you needn't concern yourself with money. What type of curriculum would you create, and why? Where would you begin? Where do you believe curriculum comes from?

Emergent curriculum begins with the child. Specifically, it begins with one particular group of children, who being young, are curious, energetic, intelligent, full of potential, and bring a wealth of prior knowledge to a classroom. The infant already knows much about relationships, the toddler is a blur of activity while figuring out how the world works, and the preschool child is beginning to learn about inquiry and problem solving on the path to becoming the ultimate researcher. When teachers work with a group of children over a period of weeks and months, they come to know those children well. They know their personalities and their quirks, their interests and their fears, their successes and struggles. Thus knowing the children and their families, teachers are given a tremendous opportunity to generate curriculum from the interests and questions of a particular group of children. This knowledge, coupled with frequent observations and carefully considered responses, allows emergent curriculum to begin unfolding.

Dreams need not be only dreams. Keeping yours in mind as you work through the day enables you to see events and routines through a different lens—one that zeroes in on what children are really trying to uncover or demonstrate in their play. It can also make you wonder what you can do in response and how you might do it.

An Invitation to Explore an Alternative

Children have a right to a responsive curriculum that is designed just for them. Deserving such a curriculum, they respond to it with engagement and delight, for it belongs to them as well as to their teacher. If you consider how much children have to offer in terms of directing curriculum, you'll be able to see a way toward a true collaboration. For instance, perhaps there is a child in your group who is full of good play ideas and leads other children. Can you help the group develop those ideas further? Or maybe you can facilitate for the children an opportunity to investigate an obscure question. Two real examples of such questions from preschool classrooms offer a glimpse of children's thinking: How does a nose know what the smell is? What is the difference between a hole and a space?

Seeing the children curious, excited, and engaged will ignite your own passion for teaching. Your job as a teacher is not to know all the answers. Rather, you must be willing to investigate alongside children, to collaborate with them as you learn together.

Emergent curriculum allows you to respect the voice of the child as well as meet standards across learning domains, and to honor unique learning styles and talents in both children and educators. If you truly believe that learning takes place during play, then you recognize that learning standards are met through relationships with materials, people, and environments—that learning is embedded in meaningful, engaging play. In your daily work, you can practice recognizing, recording, and communicating this learning. Through careful documentation, you can combine the language of play with the language of standards and articulate exactly what is taking place in your early childhood program.

For some teachers, the idea of collaborating with children in generating curriculum is not new. Those who are familiar with emergent curriculum are putting together their dream of collaborative, responsive curriculum while staying true to our society's standards for high-quality care and education. They are demonstrating that the pieces fit and the dream is possible. Within emergent curriculum, all perspectives are taken into consideration, and all players—children and adults—have a voice.

Emergent Curriculum Defined

When teachers are keen observers, when they notice not only what children are doing and playing at, but also *how* they are playing and what they are saying as they play, they are in a strong position to develop curriculum based on their observations. Throughout this book we will see how observations, transcripts of dialogue, and traces of children's work can be gathered, we will explore the process of reflecting on them to find meaning, and we will think about what the possible responses might be. Underlying these discussions are my own assumptions about emergent curriculum:

- While framed by the teacher, it is child initiated, allowing for collaborations between children and teachers, and giving everyone a voice.

- It is responsive to the child, thereby allowing teachers to build upon existing interests.

- In its practice, the teacher takes on the role of facilitator, taking what she sees and hears, and bringing to children the opportunity to discover more, dig deeper, and construct further knowledge.

- It is flexible in that curriculum planning, rather than being done well in advance, is constantly developing. Curriculum is dynamic, neither stagnant nor repetitive.

- It enables children's learning and teachers' thinking to be made visible through varied forms of documentation.

- It builds upon the theories of the recognized theorists in our field: the work of Dewey, Piaget, and Vygotsky supports the philosophy of emergent curriculum. Practices embedded in emergent curriculum make visible the work of these theorists—no longer is it contained only in early childhood texts.

An Invitation to Examine Your Practice: An Overview of This Book

As we examine what emergent curriculum means in terms of our daily practices, we will also consider the values we hold dear. When we actively consider our values about what constitutes quality curriculum for young children, we are more likely to be able to translate those values into reality in our classrooms. All too often, teachers who leave college with a set of ideals become dispirited after entering the teaching world with all of its complexities. Sometimes, even deeply held values become submerged by the practicalities of getting through the day with a group of active three- and four-year-olds.

Upon entering an organization, even seasoned teachers can be tempted to follow what's been done before. For every aspect of daily life, there is a script, a way that we commonly proceed. In this book, we will examine scripts for teaching, and ask whether we are blindly holding onto old scripts or are instead constantly developing as professionals. We will also think about how scripts for teaching can be challenged or changed, rethought or renewed, in order to provide an alternative to stale practices.

In chapter 1, we look at starting points for teachers who are beginning to explore emergent curriculum. We will meet a teacher who carefully considered her own values and then went through the process of change. She describes the challenges of rethinking her practice, and how she eventually found a good fit in terms of her workplace, thereby renewing her passion for teaching young children.

Chapter 2 considers observation as a starting point. What are you looking for as you observe, and how do you efficiently record what you see? Teachers are busy practitioners, and this chapter discusses the practicalities of observing children with curriculum in mind.

As teachers develop early childhood programs, they need to pause and think carefully, rather than blindly follow what came before. Values become a part of this careful thinking.

In chapter 3, we examine the aspects of early childhood programs that are often taken for granted: daily routines, the role of time, circle times, large- and small-group activities, diversity, and the culture of the school.

Only after some *deconstruction* can teachers think about how to reconstruct what they do in light of their values. Because most early childhood educators work in teams, they are in close relationship with each other. Decisions become collaborative, and teams must listen to each member, carefully consider, and engage in dialogue in order to make satisfying decisions about what should happen next. Such teamwork is examined through stories from teaching teams in chapters 4 and 5, as individual teachers discuss the push and pull of generating curriculum.

Chapter 6 addresses the important issue of accountability through documentation of children's learning. Early childhood professionals are responsible for developing the best possible early childhood programs and for making children's learning visible. Educators in Reggio Emilia, Italy, have introduced teachers around the world to the wonderful tool of documentation, which demonstrates the learning taking place by showing children's thinking through narratives, anecdotal notes, learning stories, tape recordings, artifacts, and teachers' interpretations. This chapter examines the many ways that teachers can make learning visible, including how to link learning to required standards.

One of the delights of emergent curriculum is that it provides an avenue for teachers to engage in classroom research. Since this approach requires consistent observation from teachers, observation and reflection soon become habitual, a way of being in the classroom. This disposition enables teachers to become researchers in their own environment. In chapter 7 we examine the stimulus of action research and how this cycle of inquiry can inform our teaching practice.

As we continue exploring the many pieces of emergent curriculum, we will reach a point where we must put all the pieces together. Chapter 8 takes an in-depth look at a long-term project, examining the starting points, the decisions that were made, the project's development over time, and how it was documented.

Chapter 9 discusses the idea of emergent curriculum as a creative act, a way to keep the passion in your teaching and to maintain collaboration with children. This chapter contains several invitations for you from the teachers in this book and from me. It is our hope that these invitations will inspire you to try something new, to step out of old scripts and into reflective practice.

An Invitation to Meet Teachers Who Use Emergent Curriculum

The Teacher's Voice stories within this book are about teachers who use emergent curriculum with varying levels of expertise or comfort. Some learned about the theories of this approach during their training and are now putting those theories into practice for the first time. Some who learned nothing about emergent curriculum during their coursework found themselves in settings where they were expected to practice it. All of them strongly believe that emergent curriculum allows them the freedom to be truly child centered while meeting the needs of their community, and they all value play as an essential vehicle for children's learning.

The teachers are employed in the following early childhood settings in the United States and Canada.

- The Child and Family Development Center (CFDC) in Concord, New Hampshire, is a laboratory school for New Hampshire Technical Institute's (NHTI) two-year associate degree program. With a capacity for forty-five children between six weeks and five years of age, the program has been in existence since 2001 and is housed in a state-of-the-art purpose-built facility. The staff at the CFDC have varied backgrounds, including training in both associate and baccalaureate degree early childhood education (ECE) programs. This lab school strives to demonstrate emergent curriculum as it is taught within the early childhood program at NHTI.

- The Ralph Waldo Emerson School for Preschoolers in Concord, New Hampshire, is a half-day preschool program serving forty families. Children are between three and five years of age, and the school is situated in a small portion of a church building. The director here is also a teacher, and the teachers have been with the school for many years. They are inspired by the practices of Reggio Emilia.

- The Peter Green Hall Children's Center in Halifax, Nova Scotia, is a full-day program that is part of a university's family housing. It serves ninety families with children from four months to ten years of age. Staff here are comfortable with emergent approaches. They are also inspired by the practices of Reggio Emilia, and some teachers have visited the Italian schools.

- The Victoria General Child Care Center, also in Halifax, was once a workplace child care center for the staff of the Victoria General Hospital. Now closed due both to restructuring of the hospital and to budget

struggles, the child care center served infants through five-year-old
children, with seventy-five families using the center for extended hours.
Many of the staff were trained in High/Scope curriculum.

In all of these stories—some of which come from student teachers in the programs described above—we will see both struggles and successes as teachers think and collaborate with children and so grow in new directions. We will hear the perspectives of teachers, teacher educators, and directors as they journey through inspiration, struggle, reflection, and renewed passion for their work.

An Invitation to Know the Author

My own experience of emergent approaches began with a childhood in British elementary school classrooms that used hands-on methods no matter what the content area. Until I began my own teacher training, I didn't realize that not everyone receives a box of buttons to work with while doing math, or that all children don't have a bin of clay in the classroom, or that every class doesn't work in small groups in which everyone is encouraged to talk! In my days in those schools, the news from the community newspapers was discussed each day, and activities were drawn from those events. I now understand that Dewey and Piaget may have had something to do with those approaches. Back then, I simply loved school and loved to learn.

When I began to work in early childhood settings as a teacher educator, consultant, and director, I soon despaired of approaches that seemed stagnant, repetitive, and certainly not centered on the child. Where was the creativity, and how did teachers display their passion? Why did activities for children have to come from books? It was in reading the works of Elizabeth Jones, John Nimmo, and Gretchen Reynolds that I experienced a moment of recognition. They discussed play-based and emergent approaches that embodied what I wanted to accomplish in working with both children and teachers: I wanted to put the children, their ideas, and their play back into the curriculum.

In working with teachers over the past twenty-five years, I have come to understand that emergent curriculum is both challenging and exciting. In my roles as college instructor and practicum supervisor, I have encountered the challenges of introducing emergent curriculum to beginning teachers who are grappling with simply surviving in the classroom. My colleagues and I have had to ask ourselves which aspects of emergent curriculum a beginning teacher could use. As the director of a lab school, I have worked with seasoned teachers who, though hired for their knowledge of emergent curriculum, still struggled with certain aspects of this approach. I am thankful for all of these experiences. Through the struggles and successes of these teachers and students, I have been able to grow in my own understanding of emergent curriculum.

An Invitation to Follow a Teacher

Occasionally during our teaching life, a moment or a set of circumstances causes us to rethink what we are doing and how we are doing it. The moment may arise as an "aha" moment while we are reading, or in a workshop or seminar, or through dialogue with other professionals. How the moment arrives is less important than what it does. For it effects change, and although change is hard (it produces disequilibrium!), it can also lead to following one's heart, to finding a good fit for one's own beliefs and values.

In chapter 1, we join Bonnie, who decided that she wanted to try an alternative approach in order to give children a voice—and did just that.

Suggested Readings

Bredekamp, S., and C. Copple, eds. 1997. *Developmentally Appropriate Practice in Early Childhood Programs,* rev. ed. Washington, D.C.: NAEYC.

Mooney, C. 2000. *Theories of Childhood: An Introduction to Dewey, Montessory, Piaget, and Vygotsky*. St. Paul: Redleaf Press.

Tanner, L. 1997. *Dewey's Laboratory School: Lessons for Today.* New York: Teachers College Press.

1

Emergent Curriculum and Your Teaching Journey

When exploring a new teaching practice, it is helpful to examine your own beliefs about early childhood education. Only then can you consider how those beliefs affect your daily work, or whether in fact they are all but invisible within the classroom.

For example, over time, early childhood professionals have coined such phrases as "play is the child's work" and "learning through play." Yet in many early care and education settings across North America, the value of play is not apparent. It is not unusual to see short time frames allotted for play or physical settings that resemble schoolrooms rather than learning environments for children under six years of age. Instead of play-based curriculum planning, one is likely to see top-down curricula designed by an authority disconnected from the particular group of children and to be implemented by following prescribed themes.

When visitors enter your classroom or center, how do they perceive your values as a teacher or director? If you want children to be able to imagine and to problem solve, to engage in complex play in order to enact their ideas and understandings, and to have a sense of agency within the classroom, you might begin by examining what your early childhood program is presently like. Then think about what you would like it to be and how you would protect and value play as a vehicle for learning within your early childhood setting. How does your curriculum for your particular group of children reflect your values, your training, and your beliefs? How does it build upon children's ideas? In what ways does it address children's developmental stages? Is it possible for you to hold on to your vision of what early childhood curriculum should be while still meeting the requirements of both society and your administration?

After many years of visiting unfamiliar classrooms as a consultant, coach, or practicum supervisor, I can gain a sense of a center's philosophy and the values its teachers hold by observing factors such as:

- **The value placed on the children's work**. This is sometimes made visible through the ways in which the work is shown, the commentary accompanying the work, and its accessibility to the children in order that they may reexamine it, add to it, or talk about it.

- **The children's engagement**. A classroom where children are truly engaged in play and exploration will not be quiet; it will be noisy and messy in a purposeful way. There will be the busy hum of active children, the sounds of materials being used, the occasional shout of joy or surprise (and yes, also of frustration or anger as children learn to negotiate), and the murmur of adults who are working with children.

- **The role of the teacher**. A child-centered classroom will have teachers who are busy, not with housekeeping tasks—although some are necessary, and hopefully will include the children—but with assisting children in finding props, chatting with them about what they're doing, quietly writing observations or taking photographs, scaffolding children's ability to work together, and problem solving with children.

- **The work itself**. An observer looking at the walls and shelves will see the kinds of investigations under way, the art, the available materials, and the accessibility of those materials, all of which tell a story—the story of what happens in this space.

Of course, any program has invisible subtleties, and a parent or other visitor would need to talk with you at length to fully understand your program. Using the preceding list, you can begin to examine your own space and decide whether or not your values are being made visible. Do you believe that open-ended materials are valuable in fostering creativity? Then your shelves should reflect this, and be stocked with interesting materials such as boxes, string, tape, and recyclables. What about respecting children's work? To examine your own values about this, look at how you displayed their work. Are the child's words included? What would happen if a child in your program wanted to build something complex and leave the structure standing? A play-based program is not without rules or structure. Rather, its structure respects the rhythms of the children as well as their interests, and fosters a sense of both order and flexibility.

Through my own experiences in early childhood classrooms, as well as through observing and collaborating with teachers and student teachers in action, I've found that emergent curriculum offers an opportunity to work with the ideas of both children and teachers, to address children's developmental needs, and to keep play-based curriculum at the forefront. It is a balancing act, certainly, and it is challenging. But challenge can be a positive and refreshing stimulus for teachers.

An Image of Emergent Curriculum

Emergent curriculum is not linear—it is organic, constantly growing and evolving. Sometimes it is even circular, as we observe, discuss, and examine documentation, raise questions, and observe again.

Unlike emergent curriculum, a book is linear in its design. We start at the beginning and move through to the end, encouraging us perhaps to think that things should happen in this particular order. Writing coherently about the process of generating emergent curriculum is difficult. The reader is likely to ask "What next?" and the answer is almost always "It depends."

Since we have as yet no device that allows us to read in a circle or a spiral with multiple entry points, an image may help us visualize the unfolding nature of emergent curriculum in order to recognize some possible beginnings for teachers. And since emergent curriculum is formed by relationships—among children, between teacher and child, within the community, and among teachers—we can wrap prior knowledge, dispositions, and relationships around the various processes of emergent curriculum, so that a more complete representation emerges.

Putting It All Together

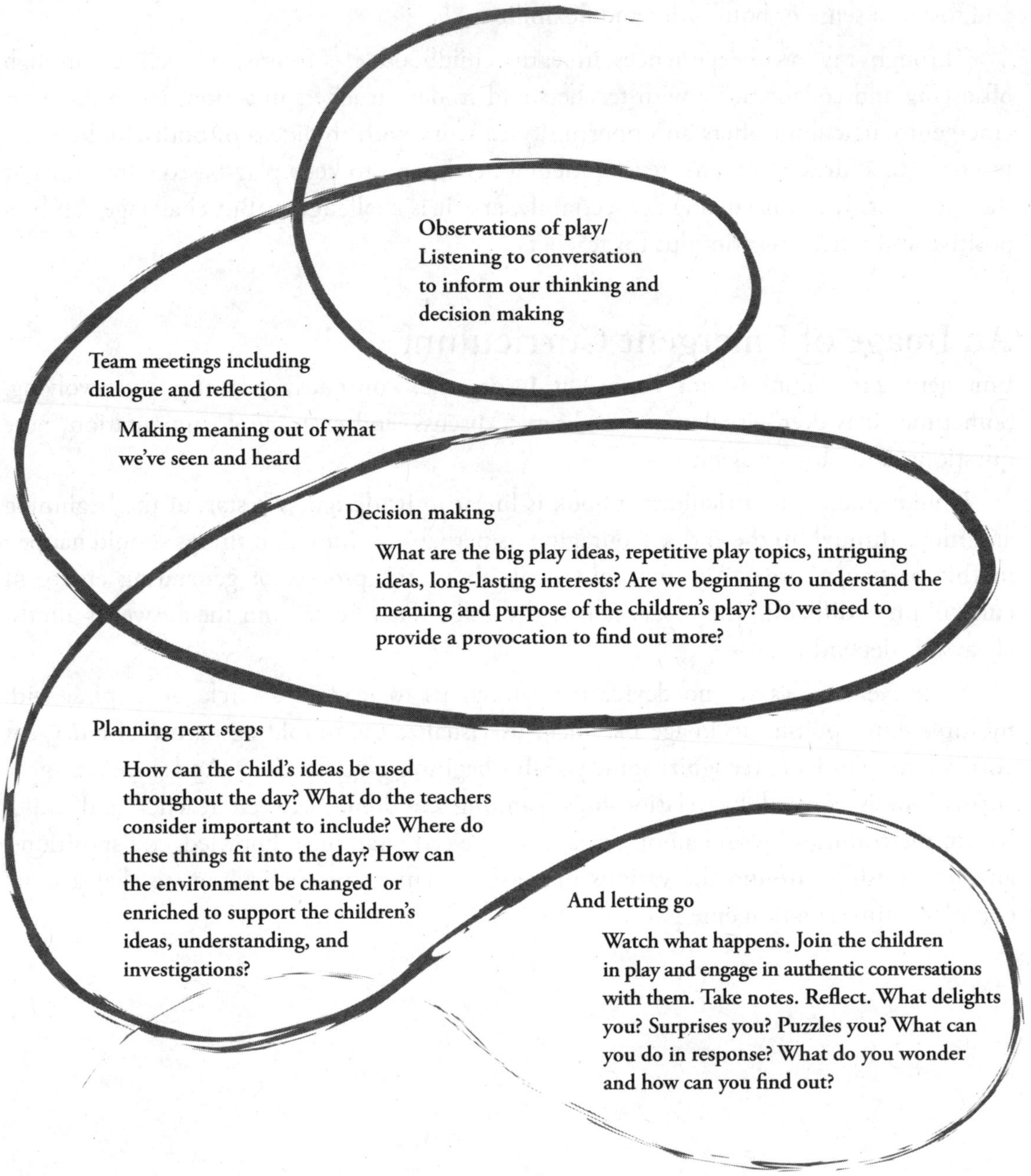

Observations of play/
Listening to conversation
to inform our thinking and
decision making

Team meetings including
dialogue and reflection

Making meaning out of what
we've seen and heard

Decision making

What are the big play ideas, repetitive play topics, intriguing
ideas, long-lasting interests? Are we beginning to understand the
meaning and purpose of the children's play? Do we need to
provide a provocation to find out more?

Planning next steps

How can the child's ideas be used
throughout the day? What do the teachers
consider important to include? Where do
these things fit into the day? How can
the environment be changed or
enriched to support the children's
ideas, understanding, and
investigations?

And letting go

Watch what happens. Join the children
in play and engage in authentic conversations
with them. Take notes. Reflect. What delights
you? Surprises you? Puzzles you? What can
you do in response? What do you wonder
and how can you find out?

By examining all the parts of this image, you can see that both teachers' and children's dispositions, relationships, and areas of prior knowledge have an effect on emergent curriculum. At the same time, you can also see the processes of generating emergent curriculum—observation, reflection, documentation, and changing the environment— and recognize that here, too, there are possible entry points for teachers.

Teacher disposition of questioning and curiosity, together with prior knowledge, experience, and intuition

Child bringing prior knowledge and experience

Observations of play/ Listening to conversations to inform our thinking and decision making

Teachers in relationship with each other, being both supportive and proactive

Team meetings including dialogue and reflection

Making meaning out of what we've seen and heard

Teachers in relationship with the child, parents, and community

Decision making

What are the big play ideas, repetitive play topics, intriguing ideas, long-lasting interests? Are we beginning to understand the meaning and purpose of the children's play? Do we need to provide a provocation to find out more?

Collaboration with the child

Teacher as researcher, child as protagonist

Planning next steps

How can the child's ideas be used throughout the day? What do the teachers consider important to include? Where do these things fit into the day? How can the environment be changed or enriched to support the children's ideas, understanding, and investigations?

And letting go

Watch what happens. Join the children in play and engage in authentic conversations with them. Take notes. Reflect. What delights you? Surprises you? Puzzles you? What can you do in response? What do you wonder and how can you find out?

Dispositions

Since, in early childhood education, we think of ourselves as being child centered, let's think further about the disposition of the child. She is a researcher, an explorer of her world. She constructs her knowledge as she handles real objects, ventures into the community, collaborates with her peers, and represents her ideas through play. Different children, of course, have different dispositions. For instance, one child may try out his ideas in a solitary way, quietly using materials over long periods of time until one day he finally makes a statement about his ideas and discoveries. Another child might be a very social learner, using the ideas of others to build upon in play, or enticing other children to help her play out her own ideas. We've all encountered the child who dives into sensory experiences, as well as the one for whom the "touch with one finger" approach feels safer. When designing curriculum, all these dispositions must be taken into account.

> The term *disposition* refers both to a person's qualities of mind and to a tendency to act or respond in a certain way.

The disposition of the teacher also has an enormous effect on what happens in the classroom. Emergent curriculum requires the disposition of genuine curiosity about children and their play. A teacher who is curious, who wonders why children are doing a particular thing in a particular way, will be genuinely interested in finding a meaningful response.

The tendency to engage in lifelong learning is another important disposition. A teacher who is willing to try different approaches, to keep abreast of new developments in the profession, and to take risks in terms of testing which teaching approaches work best is more likely to be open to the give-and-take of planning curriculum from children's interests and questions.

The disposition of the reflective practitioner is one of keeping an open mind and examining one's own practice, of taking a frequent and hard look at why things are done in a certain way, of always questioning and always thinking.

A teacher who recognizes feelings of disequilibrium as a sign of growth is likely to feel enlivened and stimulated by the process of generating emergent curriculum.

Your teaching team may include teachers who each possess one or more of these dispositions. This makes for a wonderful collaborative journey, with teachers each lending their strengths to the process. You are likely to find diversity in all teaching teams, and diversity can lead to a stronger and livelier curriculum.

Prior Knowledge

Within the image of emergent curriculum, you will also notice a reference to prior knowledge. Both teacher and child possess prior knowledge; we all come to the classroom with previous experience and knowledge of the world. The child expresses her knowledge and experiences through her play ideas, whereas the teacher demonstrates his professional expertise—and previous training—through the decisions he makes and the scaffolding he provides. Part of his professional expertise also includes his knowledge of these particular children: their development, their interests, their families, and their culture. He knows about their previous play, questions, misunderstandings, and investigations.

For example, when a five-year-old recently drew a series of straight lines and told me, "This is a phoenix," I would have been confused had I not known that she was learning Chinese characters at home. Knowing both this child and her family, I could work with her family to support this exploration at school.

Where children's and teachers' dispositions and prior knowledge meet with teachers' observations of children's interests, emergent curriculum can begin to take shape.

There are many starting points for emergent curriculum. Depending on your previous training and experiences, you may want to begin by practicing the art of observation, thereby refining that skill. Or you might reflect on your practice by keeping a journal of your own teaching and then examining how you make decisions about curriculum. To effect a change in practice, it's helpful to think about your own comfort level, the differing talents within your team, and the practicalities of how you will begin. Somewhere in the chapters that follow is the starting point that will best suit you. As you will see, the journey toward exciting curriculum is not always straightforward, but it is always engaging—for both the child and the teacher.

Describing Emergent Curriculum

Part of exploring a curriculum approach and finding a good fit for your own beliefs is to examine the important attributes of the curriculum, while keeping in mind possible starting points for your entry into the approach. Read again the list of assumptions about emergent curriculum that appeared in the introduction:

- While framed by the teacher, it is child initiated, allowing for collaborations between children and teachers, and giving everyone a voice.

- It is responsive to the child, thereby allowing teachers to build upon existing interests.

- In its practice, the teacher takes on the role of facilitator, taking what is seen and heard, and bringing to children the opportunity to discover more, dig deeper, and construct further knowledge.

- It is flexible in that curriculum planning, rather than being done well in advance, is constantly developing.

- It enables children's learning and teachers' thinking to be made visible through varied forms of documentation.

- It builds upon the theories of the recognized theorists in our field: the work of Dewey, Piaget, and Vygotsky supports the practice of emergent curriculum.

Consider, as we expand upon each point, which of these aspects you already practice, which you would like to try, and which ones you feel you could develop further. Are there approaches here that make you feel uncomfortable? If so, think about why this might be. Perhaps there will be one that raises your curiosity and makes you wonder if that's where you could begin.

Beginning with the Child

Because emergent curriculum is child initiated, observation plays a huge role. It is through observing the children at play, noticing the details of what and how they're playing, that teachers begin to uncover the children's thinking, intentions, and understandings or misunderstandings. As you discuss the play with other professionals, you attempt to find the meaning, intentions, or explorations within it. You can also plan for collaborations between children and teachers in terms of the direction of curriculum. In this way, everyone in the classroom community has a voice—the children's interests are validated and respected, while the teacher brings expertise and experience to the situation.

SOMETHING TO TRY

As you observe children playing out their ideas, try also to listen carefully to the dialogue they use with each other, and write it down for further discussion. Doing so provides an important clue to the children's understanding or misunderstanding, and to what prior knowledge they bring to the play, thereby helping you decide how to support it.

Responding to Children's Interests

Emergent curriculum is responsive to the children, thereby allowing teachers to build upon existing interests. And there are many, many interests within any group of young children. With practice and dialogue, teachers using this approach become adept at distinguishing between what may be a passing moment and what may turn into a long-term endeavor. Both small moments and long-term work are valuable, and at times you may find yourself following up on several interests at once. Some will fall by the wayside, while some will continue for the long term and become deep investigations. When we succeed in uncovering deep interests, we also learn something about teaching—we learn, over time, how to make curriculum decisions more easily, how to recognize children's big play ideas, and what kinds of ideas recur over and over again, reminding us that for the children these topics are important ideas.

SOMETHING TO TRY

When you are first attempting to respond to all of the activity of children, it can be challenging to decide what to respond to. Try coordinating your team so that each of you is paying particular attention to just one area of the room during play. For instance, if you're in the art area for the morning, you could concentrate on noticing which materials were used, how children used them, and what they were trying to represent. Then, when you return to this area after some discussion with your peers, you could focus on just this particular exploration, rather than on the whole room.

Facilitating Children's Deep Exploration

When a teacher takes on the role of facilitator, she takes what she sees and hears and offers children an invitation to discover more, dig deeper, and construct further knowledge. When a child engages in further exploration, the teacher scaffolds. That is, she brings her knowledge and experience to the situation, thinking deeply about where the child is and how she as a teacher might further the child's interest, knowledge, and engagement with the topic. Rather than telling the child what the next exploration will be, the teacher facilitates learning around what interests the child.

SOMETHING TO TRY

Think about your own experiences, knowledge, and interests. Keep these in mind as you watch children trying to understand something new or beginning an investigation of something that fascinates them. Can you match your expertise to theirs in order to more deeply engage them in the topic? For instance, if you enjoy baking bread, this would be something to share with children who play repeatedly at cooking during dramatic play. If you are handy with tools and wood, think about using this expertise in helping children to construct items they need for play.

Planning Flexibly

Emergent curriculum is flexible. Rather than being done well in advance, planning is constantly developing. Curriculum is dynamic, neither stagnant nor repetitive. Flexibility is important because the teacher must have the ability to "plan and let go" (Jones and Nimmo 1994, 12). That is, plans formulated by teachers sometimes need to be set aside in order to address what really interests the children. Children learn best through what they're deeply interested in. Routines, rather than being regimented by the clock, also need to be flexible. If children have a wonderful idea that is being played out at length, they will need extra time to negotiate, problem solve, and express that idea through play. If circle time needs to be pushed back to allow time for a complex play idea, so be it.

SOMETHING TO TRY

Try counting the number of transitions during a morning in your program. Begin with the children's arrival as the first transition and count each time they're required to change activities. It can be surprising to note how many times we interrupt play. What must this feel like to the children? How do you feel when you're interrupted in the middle of something that is important to you? With your team, examine transitions and routines, and try to reduce them to what is absolutely essential. See what happens.

Documenting Learning and Thinking

Children's and teachers' thinking within an emergent curriculum can be made visible through varied forms of documentation. Through graphic means, documentation shows the process of children's investigations and learning, enabling teachers and children to revisit the work, reflect upon it, and uncover meaning and future directions. In addition, many teachers find documentation to be a way of entering into teacher research. That is, it helps them find answers to their own burning questions regarding what children are doing and thinking and how the children might learn best. It also helps teachers see how they should proceed in response.

SOMETHING TO TRY

Next time you meet with your team or are conversing with another educator, try examining a photograph or two of children at play. If you have a question about the play, write it down, and continue observing to see if you can find the answer. If you had to describe why this play was significant, what would you say and how would you say it? Try mounting one of the photos on cardstock, together with a short narrative. Share it with the child's family, and notice how they respond.

Applying Theory to Classroom Experience

Practices embedded in emergent curriculum make visible the work of theorists such as Dewey, Piaget, and Vygotsky. Their work no longer is contained only in early childhood texts. Instead, their theories come to life within our classrooms—we begin to recognize what "constructing knowledge" and "scaffolding" really mean.

For instance, imagine a child who is struggling to keep train cars connected as he wheels a train around a track he's made out of blocks. You can see that he's becoming frustrated as the train repeatedly falls apart. When speaking of social learning, Vygotsky put forth the theory that children can learn from more experienced peers. Keeping this in mind, you could suggest to the struggling child that an older child nearby might be able to help. When children show each other what to do or assist younger children, they are scaffolding for the less experienced child.

Remembering the work of Piaget, you might use the idea of constructing knowledge through experience and hands-on work, by providing many opportunities for joining things together and using trial and error until the best method becomes clearer to the child.

Thinking of Dewey, on the other hand, you might choose to take the children out into the community to study trains in real life, to ask questions of those who work with trains, and then to represent those real experiences in classroom work. Any of these responses could be appropriate, depending on the child and the program, and all of them make use of learning theory.

SOMETHING TO TRY

When you next observe a child struggling with a material or activity, watch carefully and notice the details. What strategies does the child use to try to find a solution? As you consider how to support the child's efforts, think about the theorists you are familiar with and what they suggested about how children learn best. If Piaget were in your classroom, what might he suggest you provide in the way of materials that would allow the child to discover his own solution to a problem? What would Dewey provide in the way of real work that would support the child's learning? What would Vygotsky say you should do in your role as a more experienced partner who can extend the child's knowledge?

Recognizing Types of Play

During their training, most teachers study play in depth. Can the theories we all study be connected to what you observe children doing each day? Understanding play and the teacher's role within it helps you understand what might be happening within the play, and therefore how you might respond. Do you recognize what you're seeing in terms of different kinds of play? In a mixed-age group of children, you might observe several stages of play:

- **Exploration**. Direct knowing through exploring the physical world with the senses, physical action, and the beginnings of language.

- **Socio-dramatic play**. Constructing knowledge through dramatic, socio-dramatic, and constructive play: the self-initiated re-creation of one's experiences in order to understand them.

- **Investigation**. Experiencing and representing the world through classification, imagining with materials, structured dramatization, and developing literacy (Jones and Reynolds 1992, 3–5).

During just one morning in a preschool classroom, you are likely to observe all these stages of play. The three-year-old who is experimenting with mixing sand and water and then tries to pour the goopy result through a funnel is experiencing directly what works and what doesn't. His senses are involved, as is trial and error, and he is engaging in exploratory play. The teacher might offer other sensory materials to work with, include some language that supports the play, and give the child some tools that may work differently from the funnel: sieves, tubing, or sponges, for instance.

Meanwhile, in the dramatic play area, a four-year-old girl is taking orders for pizza. Using her own form of cursive, she writes another child's order on a clipboard, assembles a tray full of dishes, and balances the tray on one hand as she approaches the table. She's making sense of a recent restaurant experience by reenacting it in socio-dramatic play. Many props could be added to this experience (pizza tools, for instance, or menus from pizza restaurants), but there's also opportunity here to take this a step further and expand the child's knowledge of the real world through a field trip to restaurants where she can watch the people who work there.

In another area of the classroom, a five-year-old is engaged in investigating quilts. With the teacher's support, he notices that some have squares that are sewn side by side, while others are appliquéd. He is also able to pick out similar patterns in individual quilt squares, and begins organizing these similar fabrics into stacks. He is engaged in investigation, using classification and very specific language to help make sense of what he's seeing. If this interest continues, fabric squares could be offered for classification during play in a quiet area or in the dramatic play corner. If the children are specifically interested in quilting, a quilter could be invited to share her expertise in the classroom.

What you see in your own classroom during play can depend upon numerous factors: the age group you're working with, the variety of open-ended materials available to the children, the amount of time available to them, their levels of social skill, their problem-solving abilities, their creativity. How you respond to their play, however, will have much to do with your own disposition.

This journey through the processes of emergent curriculum will involve reexamining your beliefs about why you do what you do in the classroom and how you can work in collaboration with both adults and children. It will undoubtedly involve change, and change can be uncomfortable. It requires that you examine yourself and your practices, and the result can feel like a dive into uncharted waters. But the ensuing journey is likely to be exciting; it will provide you with renewed energy for doing your very best for young children. Let's step out of the box together and examine the journey of an educator as it proceeds, in all its complexity, toward a more emergent practice.

The Teacher's Voice: Emergent Curriculum and Child-Centered Practice

Before joining the staff of the Child and Family Development Center (CFDC) in Concord, New Hampshire, Bonnie worked for several years in classrooms that used a thematic approach to generating curriculum for preschool children. She had never learned about emergent curriculum in theory or used it in practice. She began her work at CFDC in a toddler classroom, and now works with preschool children. Bonnie tells the story of how she began working with emergent curriculum with toddlers, and what it felt like. She first describes working in a theme-based classroom.

> **We had preplanned themes—that is, planned by the teachers—but we never talked about how the *children* felt about what we were doing or how they reacted to what was happening in the classroom. We didn't even ask ourselves if the children were enjoying what they were doing. The curriculum wasn't cocreated. It wasn't a collaboration at all. We spent all our time trying to do *what everyone else thought we should do*: letters and calendars for the parents because that's what they'd experienced in their own childhoods, or trying to please our administrator, who wanted everything planned weeks in advance, and so on.**

Notice that Bonnie pays attention to her own feelings of discomfort. She identifies what did not feel right to her and why. Such self-awareness is a part of the reflective process. Teachers can pause from time to time to examine their practices and where they came from, noticing whether they are a good fit for their own values and whether they need to be tweaked or subjected to large-scale change. Bonnie decided she needed major change in order to make her teaching practice fit with what she believed about how children learn and how teachers should and could respect the child's voice.

This huge decision felt right to Bonnie. Like many teachers who change their practice, however, Bonnie experienced feelings of disequilibrium as she went through a period of transition in her new workplace.

> **In the first classroom I worked in at CFDC, with toddlers, I was struggling, not understanding it yet. Working in collaboration with the team during planning meetings really helped. I began to understand how they came up with a plan**

by examining observations and them talking about those observations until as a team we felt we understood what we were seeing as we tried to uncover the children's true intent. We weren't very sure of ourselves, because the toddlers were interested in exploring *everything* around them! Then one day when the director joined us, we tried to explain what was happening. I find that when I try to articulate a struggle to someone else, the answer starts to appear. There's something about talking it through that helps me to think.

What Bonnie describes is the feeling of disequilibrium that comes with change. Notice, however, that she gave herself some time. She was able to take the time to reflect with peers and a supervisor, to learn through dialogue with others. She was also able to learn some new skills through a workshop on observation. Here is Bonnie's description of "what was happening" at that time. As you read her words, think about the many directions one could take in responding to what the toddlers were doing and about those two perplexing things happening at the same time.

There's a funny thing going on right now. When I try to sing with the children a song that another teacher previously sang, they tell me: "No! That's Miss Lindsay's song!" and get very upset. And the same thing happens when I ask *them* to pick a song. If another child picks one they know, they'll say: "*My* song!" and almost come to blows over it. Also, they're into a very toddler-like trend of wanting to be *so* independent, and yet they still need plenty of nurturing. Some days they want to do everything themselves, and on other days they want us to do everything for them!

A first response to this story might be to think about toddler notions of ownership and independence, and this would be valid. The team, however, decided to step back and ask themselves some questions: "What is their developmental task right now? What does this anecdote show us about that? What are they longing for? What can we do in response?"

We began thinking about the developmental work of toddlers. It seemed to us that four things were under way: the search for independence (including routine things during the day that children would like to do for themselves); working on partnerships; cooperation and community (that is, learning to be with others in a group); and issues of ownership—always a toddler topic! If we thought of *these* things as the toddlers' curriculum, what would happen to our classroom environment, to our routines, and to the kinds of activities we were doing? With some brainstorming, we were able to come up with some ideas, such as using practical life activities (borrowed from Montessori), working side by side at the easel, and partnering throughout the day with the teachers doing routine tasks. At the same time, I started using cards with drawings (which represented songs) for making choices at circle time. We kept them in a special decorative box. The children reacted *really* well to these, perhaps because it gave them some feeling of control.

From here on, the teachers were able to construct a web of ways for making choices available to the toddlers and for allowing varying degrees of independence.

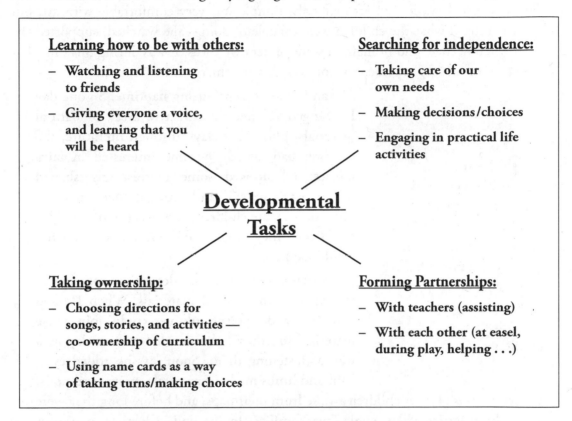

Learning how to be with others:

– **Watching and listening to friends**

– **Giving everyone a voice, and learning that you will be heard**

Searching for independence:

– **Taking care of our own needs**

– **Making decisions/choices**

– **Engaging in practical life activities**

Developmental Tasks

Taking ownership:

– **Choosing directions for songs, stories, and activities — co-ownership of curriculum**

– **Using name cards as a way of taking turns/making choices**

Forming Partnerships:

– **With teachers (assisting)**

– **With each other (at easel, during play, helping . . .)**

Can you see how far Bonnie has come? With the team, she is reflecting not only on what the toddlers want to do, but why. Team members asked themselves a question that relates back to theory—what is the children's developmental task right now? From this question, and from uncovering the answers, curriculum ideas emerged.

And then, just as she began to feel a little more comfortable, a teacher left the center and Bonnie was transferred to the preschool classroom.

I felt like a duck out of water. There were so many loose parts around! I know that this kind of equipment is essential to emergent curriculum, but I had to find my way around the room, figure out the routines, observe closely, and get to know the children before I felt that I could contribute anything at all to the team.

Bonnie found herself back in disequilibrium. She felt out of place, a little lost in this busy environment stuffed with interesting, open-ended materials for children to use. But maintaining good humor and a wait-and-see attitude, she took the time to observe and to build relationships with the children.

For Bonnie, contribution began in the art studio—an engaging, stimulating area at the end of the room that was full of enticing materials for children—from beautiful junk, to clay, and a wide variety of art materials. Bonnie was very comfortable with art, but she hadn't realized what the children were capable of doing. She watched, supported the children when needed, and brought in some of her own ideas. It was during this time that she experienced an "aha" moment of connection with emergent curriculum.

Invitation, in this context, refers to a set of materials or an activity that is set up in response to a demonstrated interest. The materials may or may not be taken up and used, depending on the level of interest. Setting up such an invitation enables the teacher to test the waters, to see if the idea is worth pursuing further.

Alexandra never slept during naptime. So one day I arranged for her an attractive array of natural materials, plus some clay. Through literature, the children had already become interested in fairy houses. I'd noticed some interestingly shaped flower petals outside and brought them in as an invitation to the children, not because of any idea about how they might use them, but to see what would happen.

Alexandra and I spent a long time together as we explored the natural materials. When I asked her, "How do you think we could join these materials together?" she decided to use clay as a way of fastening them. Soon, as she added eyes, hair, and limbs made from petals, twigs, and pods, a fairy evolved. Other children awoke from their naps, and before long they were all making fairies, then whole fairy families. In the end, a long-term project emerged.

After observing, Bonnie brought her own voice to an existing interest—fairies—and contributed something she thought might be enticing to children. She collaborated with the children, and she scaffolded Alexandra's thinking by asking a question. Not, in this case, a closed question with a correct answer, but a thought-provoking question—"How do you think we could . . . ?"

As with any in-depth project, the teaching team talked a great deal on a daily basis about what was happening, and this, too, was new for Bonnie.

Our discussions, sometimes . . . wow! They are so deep. It's a very different kind of work, very cerebral compared to what I was used to. Sometimes I jokingly tell the team that my head hurts! I'm definitely thinking a lot more, and it feels really

good. It makes me feel proud of how we research, stand back and look carefully at what the children are doing, and really think about it. For instance, how can we change things? If something doesn't work out, we can't attribute that to the children. It's for *us* to think about. What can *we* change or try differently? It's so reversed from what I was used to, and it works so much better for the children and the adults, in both a practical and an intellectual sense. Thinking back, I can see that this was what I always wanted to do, but I didn't know it!

The thing is, now that I'm in an environment that is comfortable with emergent curriculum and child-centered approaches, I'm convinced that the children I'm working with in this school are so much more engaged in learning. They are really *interested* in what they're doing. They write about it, and represent their learning with many kinds of media. They're learning about *everything*, because their interests are so diverse, and we follow up on what interests them. We have very few behavior issues, because the children are too busy with meaningful work—meaningful to *them*, and supported by *us*.

As Bonnie talks about how she now approaches her work, we can easily perceive her enthusiasm. Her disposition—an openness to change, a willingness to try new things, a commitment to learning, a tendency to engage in child-centered practices—and her curiosity led her to reflect on her original teaching practice. It also helped her understand that she needed a different approach and permitted her to follow her curiosity about how children's voices could not only be heard but made visible through curriculum.

What can we learn from Bonnie's experience? She began teaching in settings that didn't feel like a good fit for her. Her natural tendency as a teacher was to allow children to explore and create with a wide array of materials, and to collaborate with them. When the opportunity arose, she sought out a better fit for her philosophy. We can understand from her story that it's natural to feel nervous or uncomfortable with change, but that change can be very much worth the effort. It is clear that Bonnie has grown, feels more confident, and has renewed passion for her work, perhaps due to the feeling of being able to create curriculum in response to her children. Bonnie feels that she has found a good fit for her own philosophy about how young children learn; she now describes herself as a deep thinker, a researcher, and a contributor to the team. She has learned to observe along with her team and to *use* those observations to plan further steps. In order to think deeply and find meaning, we need to collaborate and engage in dialogue with other teachers (Rinaldi 2006). It is easier to "think hard" when thinking with others! And sometimes, if we notice and listen carefully, the children lead us to what to do next.

The Child's Voice: The Mapping Project

Earlier in this chapter, you read about the importance of observation, facilitation, and collaboration in creating emergent curriculum. The following project demonstrates all of these, including the teachers' tendencies to be curious about children's understandings, and to scaffold. In the preschool room, teachers notice, note, and follow up on a small beginning in the midst of a busy morning.

During a long play period in the preschool room, Sam, Norman, and John, each with a rolled-up paper in hand, approach Miss Karen. Sam says, "Miss Karen, I have a map." He unrolls the map to reveal an X, and tells her, "That's where the treasure is." As Miss Karen watches, the children walk to a small cabinet nearby, open a drawer, put their maps inside, and close it again. Then, opening the drawer with wide eyes, they say, "We found the treasure!"

Later, Karen and the other members of the preschool teaching team wondered, "What do children know about maps? Why is playing at finding treasure a recurring theme in childhood play?" As they asked the children more about their maps (What are maps for? Who uses a map? Why?) the children told them, "A map is how you find things." This gave the teachers a direction to follow in terms of what to offer the children. Could they map where to find things in their classroom? Find and represent the path to the front lobby of the school? Map their playground? These were genuine questions on the part of teachers; they didn't know the answers. So they offered several invitations to the children in the form of mapping activities to try. The children's responses would tell them what to do next.

Beginning with familiar areas of the school and working with individuals or in small groups, children and teachers began to work together on mapping. What began with a handful of children in one area of the room soon engaged the majority of the children in different ways. After discussing where they lived, some of the older children were able to represent their streets with drawings of houses or apartments. Other children, with scaffolding from a student teacher, mapped what they saw around them as they walked along the bike path in the yard—the sandbox, the rocks, the flowers. After a teacher asked, "How can we find the way to Miss Amy?" others mapped their way to the front desk in the lobby "where Miss Amy works." Familiar stories supported their thinking as they drew maps of how to get to the house of the Three Bears. And finally, after reading Sarah Fanelli's *My Map Book* with teachers, the children realized that just about anything can be mapped, and proceeded to map their hands, feet, and faces.

This project emerged humbly. It required no major event, long formal observation, or developmental milestone in order to generate curriculum. It took only an observant teacher who noticed a small moment, reflected with peers about what to do in response, and was willing to find creative ways to sustain the children's interests. Emergent curriculum doesn't have to come from complicated beginnings, but it can lead to wonderfully complex play and learning.

What Are They Learning?

Through play within the map project, children learned

- **Spatial relationships**. What is in front, behind, beside their houses? Children had to be able to represent this mentally before they could represent it graphically.

- **Mathematics**. The children had to consider distance, and how they would represent "a long way away" compared to "nearby." Here teachers had an opportunity to include measurement in many forms.

- **Representation**. How do children represent familiar routes and pathways? Do they prefer graphics, construction, or sculptural means (for example, clay) to represent what they know? These children preferred to draw maps, even though they used clay frequently in their classroom. Eventually, they were able to represent the real world in a symbolic format.

- **Emerging literacy**. Can children connect concepts from familiar stories to their own lives? This group of children understood the concept of finding things with maps. Therefore, they were easily able to draw the way to the house in the story of the three bears, a story they knew well. They also used information from a nonfiction source (*My Map Book*) to extend their knowledge about mapping, and they tried some new approaches.

- **Social learning**. This project began with play in a small group. The children continued to work with others throughout, but they also had the opportunity to do independent work (for example, mapping the playground according to what they themselves noticed). Through documentation panels, children were able to examine the work of others.

- **Language development**. New words and verbal expressions are naturally introduced throughout any project. In this case, new words often were related to spatial and mapping concepts concerning what the children were drawing: *trail, surrounded, narrow, wide, near, far,* and, of course, *X marks the spot*!

Looking back, we can connect this project to the aspects of emergent curriculum we've talked about in this chapter. A simple idea from children was noticed during play (observation) and a teacher made a short anecdotal note about what had happened (documentation). The event was then discussed and reflected upon with the team (reflection and dialogue). Exploration of maps was allowed to develop over an unprescribed period of time and was supported by teachers, who continued to watch and offer support as needed (flexibility and responsiveness to children's ideas). And throughout the whole enterprise, teachers were watching, making notes, talking, collecting artifacts, and taking photographs (documentation).

This approach is quite different from the prescribed themes that Bonnie described earlier in this chapter. We know the children were interested in this topic, since it came from their play idea. Teachers and children collaborated, and tangents that the children wanted to explore (mapping hands and feet, for example) were respected and supported. And yet, through play, learning was always present and made visible through the teachers' observations and documentation.

It is clear that in order for curriculum to be responsive to children's ideas, teachers must notice small events during play. When we're paying attention to children's play ideas and writing them down, we have many choices of directions to take.

How will this observation take place, and how do we know what to observe? What will we use and what might we safely ignore? In the next chapter, we will see that there is a point at which we begin to make decisions that reflect our values and philosophy, a place where the child's voice is protected, and where the thinking of the child and the teacher come together.

Suggested Readings

Jones, E., and J. Nimmo. 1994. *Emergent Curriculum.* Washington, D.C.: NAEYC.

Jones, E., and G. Reynolds. 1992. *The Play's the Thing: Teachers' Roles in Children's Play.* New York: Teachers College Press.

2

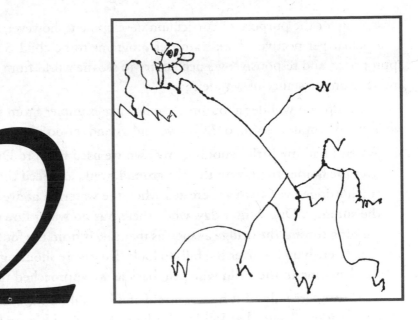

Observing to Capture Children's Ideas

As we begin thinking about the big picture of how emergent curriculum can come together, we also need to think about real classroom life. How does emergent curriculum unfold, in the practical sense, every day? When I asked classroom teachers where they begin when thinking about emergent curriculum and where their ideas come from, they shared the following thoughts on observations as a source of curriculum:

> We observe play, social interactions, misinterpretations, and then we teachers work together to come up with a creative response.

> We use a cycle of observations/dialogue/brainstorming/reflection and then interpretation.

> We provide a rich environment, and then watch and listen.

> (Stacey 2005)

Many early childhood educators are keen observers of young children. Teachers are fascinated by children, and they're trained to watch carefully, for many purposes.

Observing for the purpose of curriculum development, however, requires that we take on a particular perspective. If we want our programs to be child centered, developmentally appropriate, and responsive, we need to try to see the world from the child's point of view and take on the stance of wondering.

What do you wonder about in the following example? From the child's point of view, what do you think is going on? Can we understand, or do we need more information?

When I had my little school on my own we used to go to Diefenbaker Park just over the border to play on the playground, walk, and feed the ducks. There was a small bridge over a stream created when the waterfall above it was turned on in the summer. One winter day, when there was no water flowing, the kids started running toward the bridge as soon as they saw it from the footpath. All but one of them were hanging over the rails to look. They were shouting about something. I was listening to the child who held back as we approached the bridge.

I wondered aloud if he was afraid and he said he was. "Is there a troll under it?" he asked. I said that I didn't think so and invited him to hold my hand as we crossed the bridge. He took my hand and we started toward it. As we reached the middle, the other children begged us to look over the rail with them at the men's black dress sock they'd been clamoring about. When I asked where they thought it had come from, one of them said that John, a classroom assistant who'd recently left, had forgotten it there on one of our walks. The boy who'd held back said maybe the troll had left it.

When we got back to school, I read *The Three Billy Goats Gruff* and the children decided to act out the story. Needless to say, they took great pleasure in knocking the troll into the water, having him run away, of course leaving behind one sock. We looked for that sock every time we went for a walk, and we continued to act out and draw the story of how the sock got there. One spring day, after the waterfall was turned back on, we were surprised to discover that the sock was no longer under the water. Although we wondered where it might have gone, somehow that wasn't as intriguing a question as how it got there. I never thought I'd actually miss a sock!

Teresa Cosgrove, college instructor, Port William, Oregon

Teresa's story shows us that she and the children wondered about several intriguing ideas. Teresa wondered about a child's fears, while the child wondered about trolls. The whole group was puzzled by the appearance of the sock, and this became a continuing topic for them to think about and to combine with their prior knowledge of a traditional tale. The children's perspective is respected in the generation of this minicurriculum, and the adult has plenty to think about as she reflects on their theories.

From this example, we can see that curriculum opportunities can arrive from unexpected places. We must prepare to be responsive and open to such opportunities. Teacher decision making comes into play here, and so in this chapter we will explore how to make those decisions from the many possibilities that present themselves over the course of days and weeks.

This chapter explores several types of observations, what exactly to look for when observing for curriculum purposes, and a variety of ways to record what you're seeing. We'll also address the all-important notion of organization, because in order to use our many notes, we must be able to find them!

So Many Choices: What to Look For

During even a short period of play in a preschool room, we can see a great variety of action, many types of play and interactions, and constant exploration. Let's look at a sample of what's happening during five minutes of a typical morning play period.

Nancy, Lea, and Helen, all four years old, have moved several long hollow blocks to the center of the room and arranged them to form a square enclosure. Nancy lies on the floor inside the square, on a shaggy white rug. The other children drape long chiffon scarves over both the blocks and Nancy, to make a kind of see-through covering.

Meanwhile, Alan, who is five, has made a list on a clipboard of all the children in the room (eleven at the moment) and is approaching each child to ask "Are you here?" He then makes a mark next to their name and moves on.

In the art studio, three-year-old Alison works alone at an easel. She slowly dips her brush into green paint, presses it against the top of the paper, and watches the paint trickle down to the bottom. She repeats this action nine times before moving to the other side of the easel, where she repeats the action with red paint.

What Are They Learning?

- **Block play**. The girls are able to build an enclosure that is large enough for all three of them, and to use the blocks in conjunction with other materials.

- **Spatial relationships**. The girls know about *around* and *through;* about *inside* versus *outside* and *under* versus *over;* and about concepts of size.

- **Literacy**. Alan shows us his emerging understanding of literacy: print can be used in functional ways—in this case, for attendance. He is learning how to print not only his own name but also those of his classmates.

- **Science**. Alison is learning about how paint works. With time and access to varied materials, she will learn how liquid paint behaves on vertical paper, a flat surface, and 3-D objects. She is also learning that she can predict and control a certain type of mark on the paper and repeat it at will—important for the development of intentionality.

Nicholson's Theory of Loose Parts

"In any environment, both the degree of inventiveness and creativity and the possibilities of discovery are directly proportional to the number and kind of variables within it."

(Nicholson 1971, 30)

This sampling doesn't address all the children in the room, and it's only five minutes long. We know that throughout the day there will be dozens of scenarios such as these: dramatic play that continues for long periods, experimentation with new skills, and exploration of materials. How do we decide what to write down and respond to? While aiming to write observations that are objective and descriptive, try to keep the following considerations in mind as you observe what is unfolding around you.

What are the children playing at? Do they seem to have a repetitive idea that they keep coming back to? This is a possibility to watch for in every area of the room. Try to dig under the surface to uncover their intent. Yes, they may be engaged in playing at hospital or house, but *about what* in terms of these scenarios? Through this play, are they exploring caregiving? power? life and death? hierarchies? If you observe these repetitive play ideas on a regular basis, you're likely to discover underlying agendas. They may not be immediately apparent, but in discussion with colleagues, they may become clearer.

Listen carefully and write down the children's dialogue—verbatim! Don't be tempted to translate or edit what they say, or to correct their grammar. You need to be able to discuss and think about the children's thinking, and you can do this only if you have accurate information. Children's dialogue is one way to see into their thinking.

Watch for how children use materials. Are they sticking with one approach? Do they experiment? Do they combine materials in unexpected ways?

Watch for changes in play—changes in playmates, materials, levels of complexity, length of play, and so on. What do these changes tell you about the child, her development, and her ideas?

Ask if what you're seeing is new for this child or is old hat. If you've seen this play over and over, you may not need to write it down. Instead, wait and watch, and see what happens next. In the meantime, think about any scaffolding that may be appropriate to move the child's exploration forward.

Trust your judgment about what to write down. You know these children well, so you know what is significant for them. Remember, however, that you are observing for curriculum purposes. You don't have to wait for developmental milestones before writing. Consider everything as a possibility. If you keep your anecdotes short, you can write many of them during a one-hour play period. You'll then have a wealth of information to discuss, and that will be the time to decide whether each particular observation is helpful for curriculum planning.

Let's return to Nancy and her friends, who have built an enclosure with found materials from around the room. We need to ask some questions before we will know enough to respond to this play. Do these children act out this scenario every day? Every week? What are they saying about what they're doing? Does their conversation provide some insight into their thinking? Is there a leader with a play idea?

In this instance, a teacher might continue to write brief anecdotes as she watches this scene play out. She would need to listen carefully to the girls' conversations. If it's possible to ask some open-ended questions without interfering with their play, this would help guide her in terms of understanding the children's thinking and underlying intent. And then, with maybe a dozen short anecdotes in hand, she could venture into conversation with colleagues to consider whether a response is called for. Not every play scenario requires an instant response. We can take time to reflect!

Types of Observation

There are many ways to observe, and the method you choose will depend on the situation, the time you have available, whether you work alone or within a team, and what you are observing. The following methods are useful in observing for curriculum purposes:

- Anecdotal recordings

- Narratives

- Digital photography

- Videotaping

- Audiotaping

Anecdotal Recordings

Anecdotal recordings are a fast and easy way to record brief snippets of interesting, thought-provoking events pertaining to individuals or groups of children. They capture the essence of what happened in one or two sentences that are descriptive, yet concise: "Jessica cut up paper into small rectangles and printed a numeral on each one. She handed them out to several children, telling them it was 'time for the movie.'"

These two sentences tell us a lot about Jessica: She can use scissors effectively, she knows something about numerals and how to print them, and she has some prior knowledge about going to the movies. She also has a play idea in mind that may be worth pursuing. A teacher might talk with her about her experiences, or watch for further information. Recording this anecdote may take only thirty seconds, but the process of writing it holds the brief episode in mind for the teacher, giving her the opportunity to revisit it or share it with colleagues later. Imagine how many anecdotes one teacher could write in a day. Multiply that by the number of teaching staff in the room and you can see how quickly a wealth of information can be gathered.

Narratives

If an anecdote is something like a snapshot, then a narrative can be compared to a video—it records everything. Written over a period of several minutes, narratives include all the details about what's happening: children's play described exactly as it unfolds, and their conversations recorded verbatim. Narratives require being able to sit back and observe intensely for ten minutes or more so you can capture all the details.

When would you need a narrative? You might choose this technique if you're examining a play idea that is particularly engaging for the children or is part of a pattern that you've seen emerging. Perhaps you're puzzled about something and need more information. Ten minutes of writing can produce a surprising amount of detail to think about. It takes the cooperation of the whole team to make this happen. If one person is to sit back and write for ten minutes, the others must work harder to move around the room, engaging with children. But if you need detailed information, the team's collaboration is well worth the effort.

Digital Photography

Digital photography is instantaneous and therefore is useful when you are pressed for time. Photographs must be discussed soon after they're taken, however, or the essence of what was happening at that time can be lost. In a rushed situation, photos can help you hold on to what happened when there just isn't time to write. Keep these suggestions in mind when you are using a digital camera:

- Keep your camera on hand at all times. Interesting moments are fleeting, and you need to be quick to capture them.

- Never ask children to pose! Photographs should be natural and candid, capturing both the event and the process.

- Remember that children who aren't used to photography in the classroom may automatically turn and smile for the camera, or clamor to have their picture taken. If this happens, it is useful to explain why you are taking photographs: "I'm taking a picture of how you're building that" or "I'm photographing your work so we can remember it." Once photography has been used for a couple of weeks, children tend to ignore the camera.

- At the end of the day, or over the lunch period, edit your memory card so there will always be room for that next all-important shot.

- If you need to see a hard copy in order to get a feel for what you want to keep, print thumbnails—it's cost efficient, and it's very helpful, when making choices, to see "the whole."

- Get up close! In order to understand how children do things, we often need to see their hands at work. This calls for a close-up shot of those hands carefully attaching twig arms to a clay body, or pressing hard to join gluey pieces of cardboard together. It's easier to be unobtrusive when you're using a zoom lens.

- Show facial expressions. One way we can show how hard children work during their play is to show their thoughtful expressions—the frown, the gaze into the distance, the enraptured expression as they listen intently, the concentration as they engage in something new and puzzling.

Videotaping

Video recordings often produce background information that teachers may not have noticed at the time. What's happening in a far corner can be lost when teachers are immersed in a group of children. But a video of the whole room in action can provide wonderful context. It shows who's doing what, which areas are being used, the dynamics of each group of children as they move around and make choices, and the role of the teacher as she moves between children. When you're working alone, video can be your observer so that you can later reflect on what happened during play. Also, camcorders are becoming smaller and cheaper. Direct-to-DVD camcorders are a more expensive option, but they offer incredible convenience, since no transferring of video files is required. Rather, you can remove the mini-DVD from the camera and play it directly on a DVD player. The recordings are shown in scenes, so again your particular focus is easy to find.

Audiotaping

Writing down children's dialogue is quite difficult. They speak quickly, and often they all talk at the same time! Therefore, audio recordings can be very useful. Digital recorders are tiny, use no tapes, can be programmed to hold several files, and are fairly inexpensive. They are also unobtrusive, so placing one near the children's play won't attract their attention. When reflecting with your colleagues, it's helpful to hear the dialogue as it actually happened. And when you want to reflect on your own teaching, it's useful to listen to your own input during play or group time. What do you like about what you did, for instance, or what would you like to change?

Getting Ready for Observation

To make ongoing observation function smoothly, the classroom must be organized with observation in mind. Early childhood educators are wonderful at multitasking; we couldn't survive if we weren't. On any given day, we simultaneously plan for and maintain the classroom environment, engage the children in rich play and developmentally appropriate activities, support families, communicate with our peers, and document our work. At the same time, we're solving disputes, modeling social skills, facilitating learning, monitoring the bathroom, and keeping children safe and happy. For observation to fit into this busy scenario, it has to be made simple and effective.

Classroom Tools for Observation

Small pieces of paper for notetaking are essential. But since small pieces of paper tend to get lost or end up in pockets, they have to be organized in order to be useful. Consider the following ideas, all of which have been used at one time or another by teachers who observe regularly for curriculum purposes:

- **Sticky notes**. Available in sizes large enough to hold several sentences, sticky notes can be gathered anywhere (on a wall, a clipboard, or even the side of the microwave!) until you're ready to use them in a meeting.

- **Baskets**. Placed on the counter, a basket makes an attractive and convenient receptacle into which you can drop a note as you pass by.

- **Holding files**. If you create a holding file for each child's work, you can keep the files on a shelf in the classroom ready to receive notes and work samples. Placing notes directly into the file saves the extra step of filing at a later time.

- **Clipboards**. Although you cannot easily carry clipboards around when you're actively engaged with children, you can place one in each area of the room within easy reach. Seven or eight clipboards, each holding multiple observation forms, can be used throughout the day and gathered up for team discussions when needed. One of the greatest advantages of clipboards is the space they provide for writing a collection of anecdotes that take place in a specific area and for writing down the questions that crop up as you work there with children. You can design a special observation form to use with your clipboard that allows for comments. Here's an example taken from the clipboard in the dramatic play area of Concord's Child and Family Development Center (CFDC):

Dramatic Play Area	Questions & Notes to Self
Anders enters the dramatic play area and says, "I'll be the Dad." He picks up the baby doll, and says, "You need a shot at the doctor's." He pretends to be the doctor and gives the baby a shot. Then he goes back to the "dad" role and takes the baby home and cooks breakfast.	It was interesting to see that Anders took on both roles; doctor and dad. He was able to differentiate between the two. I wonder if he has recently been to the doctor himself, and experienced a shot, or perhaps his baby sister was the patient and he was observing. How many roles can a child take on during one play scenario?
Mary coos in motherese as she talks to a baby doll.	

So we have some ways to begin writing observations for the team to think about, something to respond to. As emergent curriculum evolves, we must also find a way to write down what has happened, the teachers' thinking, the decisions they made, and what happened next. We are, after all, accountable to parents, our licensing body, and our colleagues. We need to show the bigger picture of what we're doing so that everyone not only understands the learning taking place but also can contribute ideas, comments, and questions. When the children's and teachers' work is shared as it evolves, there will be a widening of collaborators, a recognition of the value of the work, and an opportunity to think together (Jones and Nimmo 1994; Fraser and Gestwicki 2002). Writing down the plan is discussed in chapter 5. For now, let's consider one of the most important starting points for observation and emergent curriculum—small moments with children that arouse our curiosity.

The Teacher's Voice: First Steps in Writing Down Emergent Curriculum

At Beech Street Preschool in Halifax, teachers were used to observing children and responding to those observations by enriching the environment or providing further activities or play opportunities. They had not, however, been able to find a way to write down their responses in a way that worked efficiently. They understood the cyclical nature of emergent curriculum and wanted to represent that process but also had the common problem of finding enough time to write down what they wanted to do in the classroom each day.

During a team meeting that I facilitated, they had the opportunity to look at ways that other teachers had overcome this problem. Examining the format developed by the preschool staff at CFDC, Janette and Holly saw possibilities.

JANETTE: I like how this format actually uses the observation; it's right there. One can see the flow of what's happening, and why, and then there's the continuity from one day to the next.

HOLLY: Yet there'll be lots of observations to respond to.

JANETTE: Yes! You alone could write a book with all your observations!

SUSAN: Here's where the teachers' voices come into play. From all those observations, you can make a decision together about which one or two to use—remember, as well, there's going to be a form like this for each area of the room, so you can respond to quite a lot across the whole preschool.

JANETTE: You know, as I look at this, I think it's quite comprehensive. It would satisfy licensing requirements, I think, but it does show the nature of how things emerge. And it covers each area of the two rooms, so we'll have lots of options for how to respond.

HOLLY: We could choose which observations to respond to at the end of each day, and then the set-up person in the morning would have a reference.

JANETTE: And then I won't have to depend on memory to think about what happened before. It will, mean, though, that we'll need lots of stuff on hand to pull out of the closet to help support the children.

SUSAN: That's true, and it's not toys we're talking about here—it's things like recyclables, string, pulleys, hardware supplies—really interesting odds and ends.

JANETTE: After years of operation, we should have a lot of that in the closets by now!

This simple example of searching for a solution demonstrates the power of collaboration between teachers—even those who've never met. Those who practice emergent curriculum sometimes have similar struggles with the practicalities. But when teachers share their expertise (and with computer use, a network of like-minded people is easy to build) then solutions appear. Teachers who are open to feelings of disequilibrium will not stop trying new approaches. Rather, they will seek out information and dialogue with others in order to continue learning.

The Child's Voice: Beginning with Ordinary Moments

A curriculum direction often comes from a simple moment spent in conversation or play with a child, a moment that makes us pause and reflect. The term "ordinary moment" used in this context was coined by Dr. George Forman, who said, "I propose that the best moments are the ordinary moments, the small and simple rather than the large and complex. Indeed, once you pause to reflect on an ordinary moment, you will discover more of the real child than occurs through a review of a dozen peak moments. . . . I will propose that ordinary moments should define our relation to the child and our success as teachers" (Forman 2000).

If as teachers we take on the stance of noticing, we'll see many moments that are worth reflecting upon. Here are two examples of brief moments during a busy play period. The first concerns three-year-old Hannah.

Hannah is working in the art area with collage materials of her choice: glue, tape, buttons, markers, and paper.

Passing by, I notice her work and sit down for approximately two minutes to watch. Without my asking, Hannah says that she is making a face with eyes, nose, and mouth.

SUSAN: So, can those eyes see you?

HANNAH: [As she takes another button.] When I cover them up with this one, they can't see anymore.

SUSAN: Oh, so if they're not covered, the eyes can see?

HANNAH: Yes. [She takes more buttons from the shelves and tapes them onto her paper.]

SUSAN: You said that those buttons were eyes. What are the other ones about?

HANNAH: When you take the tape off them, they can see.

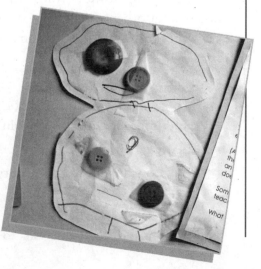

Although I wasn't a teacher in this room, I quickly wrote an anecdote about this exchange and passed it along. The teachers' conversation in response to the documentation could have veered in many directions, including a study of eyes, faces, and so on. Since these kinds of studies had been quite common in this classroom, the teachers decided to dig a little deeper. They focused on perspective taking, and they reflected on these questions:

- What does Hannah show us about her understanding of the body? What are her misunderstandings?

- How does she represent what she knows?

- To what extent can a child "see" through another's eyes? From a different perspective?

- In what other ways can we stretch Hannah's thinking and discovery in this area?

They wondered whether Hannah was developing ideas about how the physical body works and if she could represent her ideas with multiple materials. She may not have thought about what the eyes can see until Susan posed the question, and her thinking was a little confused as she tried to figure things out from this perspective. Thinking about how to scaffold this developing knowledge, the teachers decided to play with Hannah when she was in the dramatic play area. They knew they would need more mirrors to experiment with as Hannah studied eyes. In order to gain more information about Hannah's understanding, they came up with the idea of turning a doll away from themselves and asking her, "What can the doll see now?" They could then document her responses, and those of other children, in order to think about what to do next.

They also decided that in the classroom as a whole, they would respond with materials and activities around the concept of perspective taking: mirrors in front of and behind things, looking at items from beneath and above, activities in which a child could think about what others might see, exploring ways to figure out what others are feeling, and so on. All of this came from a moment or two of conversation that so easily could have been missed in a busy classroom.

Here is another example.

Nancy is drawing at the writing table. I already know that she is an enthusiastic experimenter with print. I join her, and a conversation unfolds.

NANCY: This is my cousin.

SUSAN: Can you tell me a story about your cousin?

NANCY: Sometimes she wants the dress-up clothes that I have. She wants the wedding dress. Then I tell her I'm not done with it. Then, when she takes it away and she doesn't talk to me, I don't talk to her, cuz that's taking away

mean. Then when she gives it back, I talk to her then. Now, you tell me a cousin story! [I've been writing down Nancy's story. At this point, she leans over and takes my pen.]

SUSAN: My cousin's name is Marilyn. [Here, Nancy pauses and looks at me questioningly.]

NANCY: What letter does that begin with?

SUSAN: M. [Nancy writes an M, upside down.]

SUSAN: My cousin's legs don't work, so she uses a wheelchair. [Nancy draws a chair, and then a person "in" the chair.]

NANCY: There she is, in the chair!

These five minutes spent at a table with Nancy tell us a great deal about her literacy development, her curiosity, and her understanding of social interactions. For example, as Nancy finished dictating her story, she asked for a reciprocal story, confidently took the pen, and assumed the role of scribe. Seeing herself as competent, she was willing to take a risk with writing. She also used another representational tool—drawing.

After reflecting on how to respond, the team chooses a direction. This time, they will respond with a change to the environment. They will make materials available in the writing area to encourage children to write stories: bookmaking materials, minibooks of plain paper, family photographs to use as prompts for conversation. The teacher in this area also will be watching and listening for family stories that the children may want to dictate, and she will encourage children to record their stories. Perhaps there will be some opportunities to explore diversity among families.

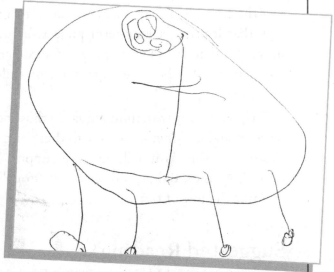

The process of observation—noticing, documenting, and reflecting on small moments spent interacting with individual children is valuable because this practice puts teachers in touch with a child's thinking. When you notice the small details of a child's play, you can make your conversation with the child specific and authentic.

Teachers who think on their feet can ask thought-provoking questions that not only further the child's understanding of what is happening but also their own understanding of the child's thought processes and construction of knowledge.

We can see from these examples that a teacher's disposition comes into play even during passing moments. When a teacher is inclined to notice small details as she passes by a child at work, she has something to reflect on and respond to. Until I stopped for a moment to watch and to listen, I had no idea what Hannah was thinking. Curiosity enables teachers to wonder, to engage in conversations with children, and to reflect on those conversations. The idea of prior knowledge is made visible through Nancy's work. Knowing something about the child, her interests, and her experimentation with print was my prior knowledge. Nancy's prior knowledge is also visible and it enabled me to collaborate with her, using print.

At the beginning of this chapter, we examined a five-minute scan of the classroom. Such quick observation and writing anecdotes about the whole is also valuable, but for different reasons. When teachers look at a room in its entirety, they see the big picture—the flow of the room, the way it is used, and the relationships. In other words, they see the context of the children's work and play. Context is equally useful and yet different from our individual work with children. And both are important. By noticing both the big picture and the details in ordinary moments, teachers can achieve a fine balance in planning their responses to children.

The examples in this chapter show us that while teachers are sometimes able to observe play that leads to a long-term project or investigation, they can also use brief, simple moments that are in fact quite extraordinary. Within the bigger context, these small vignettes give teachers a glimpse into the child's thinking and, with reflection, lead us to next steps.

As we proceed with thinking about those next steps, let's slow down for a moment. Both teachers and children need time to think and explore options. Yet in our early childhood classrooms, time is usually in short supply. Why? What makes us feel so rushed as we hurry both the children and ourselves through the day? Let's step away from routines and examine the role of time.

Suggested Reading

Curtis, D., and M. Carter. 2000. *The Art of Awareness: How Observation Can Transform Your Teaching.* St. Paul: Redleaf Press.

3

The Role of Time

Although we may not be conscious of it, we all use "scripts" in our everyday living. Take, for example, the script we enact when we go to the grocery store: we enter, find a cart or basket, walk up and down the aisles making our choices, load our groceries onto the conveyor, watch as they're scanned and bagged, and pay. Or consider an early childhood routine—for example, what children need to do in order to transition to going outdoors: they must visit the bathroom, go to their cubby and find their belongings, put on their clothing in a certain order (especially important in cold climates when dealing with the complication of snowsuits!), and wait for an adult to be ready to go outdoors with them. Typically—and sometimes without teachers even realizing it—teachers' use of time plays a huge role in how such everyday scripts unfold.

How does the idea of scripts relate to curriculum? Imagine yourself as a teacher in your first week of work in a new position. Entering the classroom in those first days, you would probably take the time to observe how things work here. You would learn the scripts for how the teaching team proceeds through the day and try to answer these and other questions for yourself as you observe:

- What is the general order of events throughout the morning and afternoon?

- How much time is spent in play?

- How is the environment provisioned to support play?

- How do teachers guide children from one activity or routine to another? How many transitions are there in total?

- How do teacher-led activities fit into the day?

- How do teachers make decisions?

All classrooms have scripts for working with young children. Scripts help teachers maintain an orderly environment, and they provide consistency and psychological safety for young children, who like to know what to expect next. They also control what kind of curriculum can unfold. In fact, familiar scripts and routines can be so strongly entrenched that they seem to have a life of their own; they can gather momentum and take on huge importance within early childhood programs. What we need to remember is that scripts for early childhood programs are not set in stone and do not have to relate to the clock. They can be examined, discussed, rethought, and possibly changed.

If you are a beginning teacher, you are not likely to sweep into a new workplace and attempt to change things. You will need to build relationships, discover your own comfort level and the rhythms of the children, and then reflect with the teaching team. But even for seasoned professionals in familiar classrooms, reexamining old scripts over time is worthwhile. Why do we do this particular thing at this time? Why do we do it at all? Do the routines serve the children well? Do they accommodate the children's rhythms? This chapter will help you ask, and answer, questions like these.

Many a daily routine or activity exists only because the person before us "did it this way." And that is simply not thoughtful enough. In carefully constructed programs, everything is done for a reason that has been considered, examined carefully, and discussed among colleagues. We construct curriculum or plan routines in a particular way because, after reflection, we think it's the absolutely best way for this particular group of children and their unique interests, cultures, and developmental abilities.

In what follows, we will take a close look at some events that typically occur in early childhood programs. Rather than accepting that "this is how it's done," however, we will use a critical eye in reexamining these scenarios. We will also think about what these events are really about and whether they might be valuable in your program. Early childhood programs do not all have to look the same; rather, they should be developed to be meaningful for the group they serve. In this chapter, we will look at the role of time in three common elements of the classroom routine: play, circle time, and meals. Then we will examine some ways to release the stranglehold the clock often has on early childhood programs.

Play

One area of the day that every early childhood educator must think about, particularly when using emergent curriculum, is time for play.

Emergent curriculum places extremely high value on play as a generator for curriculum. Play provides an opportunity for children's exploration, problem solving, incubation and development of big ideas, and, therefore, learning. It also provides the teacher, as researcher, a prime opportunity to watch and listen carefully in order to generate further understanding of the individual child. All of which means that for children to fully develop their ideas and for teachers to watch, interact, and write notes, a generous amount of time must be allotted to play.

In the United States and other western countries, we live by the clock. We feel lost when we forget to wear our watches or have to switch time zones. For children in early childhood settings, the danger lies in being so overscheduled with short time frames that there's little time for complex play ideas to unfold. Consider Alex, for instance, a three-year-old who wants to play out his first visit to the movies. He must set up the movie environment with chairs and find some friends to be the audience. This will require some negotiating, and he may have little experience with gathering other children to play. That will take time. Then a child who is more experienced with moviegoing mentions the need for tickets. They must be made. This will take more time and negotiation. Who will do what? What will the tickets say? Then there's the challenge of paying. How much will tickets cost? Is play money available in this classroom, or do the children need to make some? All of this takes place before the children even consider what movie they will watch! And the scenario may require an hour or two of free time to unfold. How many programs provide this amount of time for play ideas to develop, much less believe that doing so is necessary, worthwhile, and possible?

The teacher who is observing this play has some important decisions to make, and her response will, in part, depend upon the routines that have been established in the classroom. Putting yourself in the position of this teacher and imagining this is taking place in *your* classroom, ask yourself the following questions as you consider the example:

- Is your program set up so play periods have a distinct beginning and end? Can the routine be changed so the play period has no specified times?

- If you want to make a change to the routine—for instance, provide for a longer play period—how can you do so? Must you obtain permission, or do you have the autonomy to do that? Frequently, teachers feel that they cannot make changes in routines, when in fact nothing but a *perceived* roadblock or need for permission is stopping them. It is often possible to negotiate for change.

- Is your program play-based? If so, how are you showing that you value play? How can your routine and your flexibility toward that routine demonstrate your commitment to play? This is a big commitment, and it will affect the way that you approach your day and make your decisions.

Circle Time

Let's examine another familiar script for early childhood educators: circle time. If we visited a dozen different preschool programs across North America, we'd be likely to find a dozen different ways of conducting circle (also called large-group gathering) times. Here are two examples:

At the Ralph Waldo Emerson School for Preschoolers in Concord, New Hampshire, children meet in a large circle upon arrival. There are greetings, and parents might or might not stay for awhile. There are songs, fingerplays, and a story, all relating to the children's present interests, which are varied: the newly falling snow, saying good-bye to fall—and Japanese restaurants! There's also time for conversation—respectful, leisurely conversation during which the children talk about their families and what they did on the weekend. All three teachers sit with the children and support the children's ability to listen to each other and ask questions. When the children show signs of restlessness, circle ends. In September, when the children are new to the school, each of these components is kept very brief, with circle time perhaps totaling ten or fifteen minutes.

Depending on the children's development and tolerance for being in a large group, this meeting may extend in the spring to perhaps twenty minutes or more. There is always *action* interspersed with listening and talking. Circle time moves at a thoughtful pace that is responsive to the children's needs. What happens next depends on what the teachers have observed, for they then tell the children about their observations: "Yesterday I saw so many of you using the zoo animals in the block area! Today you'll find some baby animals there, because yesterday Sara and Paulo were playing animal families." The children leave the meeting in a leisurely manner, using a song, accompanied by guitar, that mentions each child's name. As they hear their name sung, they leave to explore the carefully provisioned environment. After choosing what to do, they spend an hour or more in play.

From this example we can see that the teachers at this school know a great deal about child development and that they are attuned to what children of this age want and need. Three- and four-year-olds are not able to sit for long periods of time, and here they aren't required to. Still egocentric, they of course need the opportunity to talk about themselves. This is done in a casual and natural way—in conversation, rather than in turn taking, which would be excruciating with twenty-one children. Some of the children also need a longer good-bye with mom or dad, and this is welcomed. We can feel a sense of respect, gentleness, and fun in this circle time. The pace is varied, as is the content. No time for boredom here. The children are soon off to explore the possibilities for play, which are briefly explained to them.

Perhaps you've seen circle times unfold in a different way, as in the following example:

> At another preschool, circle time occurs in the middle of the morning, although the teacher waits for a lull in the action before asking children to tidy up. Once most (but not all) the children are seated in a circle, they begin with a familiar greeting song, and then the teacher asks the children to choose other songs. They are enthusiastic about singing, often moving to the music, and the singing lasts for about fifteen minutes. Children who were still tidying up come to join the others as they finish. The tone and the pace are relaxed, yet playful. Then one of the children notices that big fluffy flakes of snow are falling outside. After the initial excitement, the teacher asks the children to listen to the snow. She opens the window, and silence follows as the children are mesmerized by the quiet and the slowly falling flakes. For a few moments, the teacher's plans are put on hold. She had a language experience planned, with chart paper nearby. But instead of playing with rhymes, she invites the children to tell her some words that describe the snow and writes these down in a list for the children. Later, they use this list to make a book about this first snowfall.

These examples show that circle times can be quite different. In the first setting, the purpose of circle time is not only to welcome the children and their families but also to set up the day. The children's previous work is both noted and connected to what will happen on this day. There is a conscious effort to be relaxed and at the same time efficient in setting the tone for the play to come. In the second example, teachers have made a conscious effort to avoid interrupting engaging play, and they are relaxed about when exactly each child joins the circle-in-action. It is clear that these decisions have been reached by teachers after discussion about what they value and what circle times are for in their particular settings.

We can ask further questions about these circle times: How do each of these gatherings address children's developmental stages and needs? How are the children's interests incorporated? What are the rights of the child at circle time?

Like all aspects of our daily routines, circle times have scripts, and those scripts need to be examined on a regular basis. Your own beliefs about this type of routine will be influenced by several factors: your training, reading, professional development, and the requirements of your school. But what do you believe about this familiar type of gathering? What is circle time for?

SOMETHING TO TRY

Take a few days to pay attention to your own circle times or morning meetings. How do the children respond to this regular gathering time? What does this response tell you? Are you happy with circle time, or is this a time of day that needs to be rethought?

For instance, it's possible that in your setting, circle time may best be conducted with smaller groups of children rather than the whole group. This would require less waiting for turns during discussions or games, more one-on-one attention, and less focus on the troubling behaviors that can occur when children are in large groups. Or, if your school values the coming together of the whole group, you might consider a circle full of physical action, with less emphasis on sitting.

Meals

Just as adults eat when they are ready, so children need to listen to what their bodies tell them about hunger. Newborns are very efficient at this; they cry, and we feed them! It isn't long, however, before young children find themselves on adult schedules for eating. While there is nothing wrong with eating three meals a day, it's also important for children to be able to eat when they are hungry rather than when someone tells them to. With this in mind, some centers offer an open snack, when food is offered for a period of about forty-five minutes in the morning. During this time, children make the decision about when they will eat. Some children come right away, and some choose to finish what they are doing before breaking for a snack. Others choose to wait for a friend to eat with, delaying their snack until their friend is ready. And, of course, some children choose not to eat, perhaps taking just a drink of water or juice instead.

This openness and flexibility toward snack is valuable in several ways:

- Children eat when they are hungry, thereby learning to attend to their bodies' cues.

- Food is not wasted, since it isn't portioned out and presented at a time when the child isn't interested.

- Children have some feeling of control and decision making.

- Children who choose not to snack usually eat very heartily at lunchtime.

It is easier, of course, to organize a flexible and open snack than to do the same at lunchtime, when hot food is often served. But with effort and commitment, teachers can at least vary the time when lunch begins, in order to tune in to children's rhythms. If they have eaten a good breakfast and a snack, not all children are ready to eat at noon. What can be done about this? In what ways can teachers and the children in your classroom think about lunchtime differently? Can there be two lunchtimes available for children? If staffing makes this impossible, can the children at least choose the size of their servings and serve themselves? Eating family style, with bowls of food and manageable serving spoons, is another way that children can make their own decisions about how much they eat.

As with all decision making about routines in early childhood, it is the *manner* in which it's accomplished that is important. Have previous decisions been based on observations of children and their responses to the routine? Ask yourself whether the routines in your setting are organized around the real rhythms of the children or instead follow old scripts or adult schedules. If you're willing to reexamine routines, then by using observations, conversations with children and colleagues, and a willingness to try something new, you will be able to reinvent the classroom day so that there's a natural flow that is tailored to the children in your care.

Untiming the Curriculum

The clock exerts a powerful control in the public school system. A bell rings, and everyone changes lessons or classrooms or tasks. Unfortunately, some centers for young children are effectively run by the clock. Think about how your day might change if you and your team members took off your watches. How would you know when to change activities? What would you use as your cues?

As you consider this idea—and it will feel radical to anyone who depends heavily on a watch to organize the day—think about alternate ways that you could make decisions about what's going to happen next in your classroom. For example, when you are deciding whether to create a transition to a new activity, ask yourself some of these questions:

- Is the children's play winding down or are they still deeply involved? Are they full of ideas for what to do next? Are you willing to allow them to play out these ideas?

- How is their energy level? Are they full of vigor and playing robustly, or are they lethargic and needing a break in the action?

- Are the children hungry or thirsty? How do you know?

- Rather than ending it, could you take what the children are doing now and continue it as part of your next activity? For instance, if it's impossible for the children to play out their idea of building a zoo right away, could circle time be spent in brainstorming and assembling props for the next day's zoo play?

- How long have the children been playing? If it's been less than an hour, take a good look at what the children have been doing and ask yourself if they've had enough time to think through and act upon their ideas. Have they been supported in their play? Do they understand that they can take more time and get more props if they need them?

Sometimes we continue with familiar practices because we are comfortable with them. Then, when we're asked to try something new, everything is thrown into disarray—until a new way forward appears. We look next at what happened to two teachers who decided to take off their watches.

The Teacher's Voice: Removing Clocks from the Classroom

Tanya and Elizabeth were teachers of a group of eight toddlers eighteen to thirty months of age in a Halifax child care center that valued developmentally appropriate practices. When they began working together, the morning routine included free play (about thirty minutes), circle, small group, snack, outdoor time, story, and lunch. With the teachers trying to keep things "on time," the pace was rushed and there were lots of transitions. Although Tanya and Elizabeth were skilled teachers who could keep the routine smooth with little waiting time, free play (the portion they agreed was most important) was disappearing due to time constraints. Then one day, these teachers removed their watches, as well as the timepieces from the classroom. And everything changed.

Below, using excerpts from the teachers' journals, we follow the experiment as it played out.

It's been a month since I began this toddler project. It's thrilling to be introduced to planning through the interests of the children as well as not having any sense of time.

The feeling of being thrilled didn't last long, however. Over the next few weeks, the formal program disintegrated. The teachers became so focused on what the children were doing that other components of the day simply didn't occur. Circle disappeared because the children were focused on their play. The staff didn't want to interrupt the children for small group. Outdoor play sometimes didn't occur until the afternoon. The teachers complained of feeling "adrift" and feeling that "nothing was happening." And one teacher was so focused on the children's play that the other felt compelled to complete all routine chores—housekeeping, diapers, hand washing, and so forth. She didn't appreciate this change in responsibilities!

As time went on and the teachers became increasingly alert to the children's activity and thinking, the rushed feeling in the classroom disappeared. In spite of this change, the two teachers often disagreed in their interpretations of the children's needs and interests. They discovered that they had to renegotiate how to make decisions about when to switch to another activity; previously, the clock had decided for them.

> The most difficult thing is making a "together decision" about what should happen next in our day. Today, a few children and I were playing with materials, and the others were ready for some gross-motor activity. I asked Elizabeth to go ahead with the gross motor without us, and we'd join them when we were ready. I knew the children with me weren't ready to tidy up yet, and I wanted to try not doing everything together. We can separate things and still make it work.

Here we see an important shift in Tanya's thinking. She is experimenting with what for her is a new idea: to split the children into different activities. And why not? Children of all ages who are in full-time child care surely must tire of being in a large group all day long.

Once the clock no longer dictated Tanya and Elizabeth's work patterns, a new curriculum began to emerge. Its focus was not what the teachers believed was "good" for the children. Rather, the children began to co-own the curriculum with the teachers. Observations were more astute and precise and more cohesively tied to programming. And the teachers continued to experiment with the order of events during the day.

> If we could have circle when everyone arrives instead of before lunch, it would give the children a chance to say hello and talk with each other. . . . They have a hard time with circle after outside time, because they're full of energy and don't want to sit down when they come in. Circles first thing in the morning may even give the children a chance to grasp an idea for play for the remainder of the morning. It would also mean fewer transitions. Oh, I do think this is going to work!

After a beginning full of disequilibrium, we can now hear the excitement in the teacher's voice. Through the process of reflection and experimentation and dialogue with her partner, she has found a new way of thinking about the morning routine, and she is moving forward into a new practice in response to the children. After trying out her idea for a new time for circle, Tanya went on to say:

> Circle went great. We talked about flowers growing, dandelions and so on, and pretended to move like flowers blowing. When outside, we looked for flowers and picked dandelions. The interest taken from circle was brought outside, and it lasted through the whole day. Wow.

Tanya and Elizabeth's experience is described in full in the article reproduced at the end of this chapter. Even from this small excerpt, however, we can see that when we take timepieces out of the formula for making decisions, things change dramatically. Suddenly we are required to make decisions based on other criteria: what the children are doing, their level of engagement, their interests and our ability to follow up on them, their energy level, and so on. When generating emergent curriculum, we must take every opportunity to reexamine the familiar in light of what we actually observe in the moment. Forcing ourselves to pay less attention to the clock is one way of achieving this.

What does it feel like to be a child in a clock-controlled environment? Or in an environment where there are so many transitions that the children become disoriented?

Sometimes the children's actions rather than their words speak for them. In the following example, toddlers are again the focus, but this time it is their behavior that forces a change in the use of time.

The Child's Voice: Children's Reactions to Transitions

In the following story, Lisa Ranfos, director of the Child and Family Development Center, comments on the struggles taking place with the toddlers in the family room. This room had fourteen children between the ages of eighteen months and three years, and three staff members. These children were only just beginning to develop language, and therefore could not fully express their wants and needs.

Over a period of about three months, there were times during the day—particularly during transitions—that felt chaotic and resulted in physical reactions from the children. Biting and pushing, as well as temper tantrums, were not uncommon. After some observation, Lisa described the teaching team this way:

> **They were stuck in a period of following behaviors to change the environment, instead of following the interests of the children to be proactive in creating invitations that would invoke curiosity and interest. The children seemed confused and each transition became a battle. Instead of looking at the proactive side of planning for curriculum, it was as if the staff were so scared of the behaviors (from family feedback and pressures) that they created *more* transitions, thinking that these would help the children. This kept the program in a cyclical pattern of negativity.**

When considering routines and their effects on behavior, it's helpful to use the objective eyes of an observer. Someone from the outside—the director, another teacher, or a visiting consultant—can see the situation clearly rather than being immersed within it. In this case, Lisa could see that when the teachers imposed more transitions rather than offering invitations for activity, the toddlers resisted by being unwilling to move from one part of the routine to another.

Lisa quickly realized that the team needed help. She asked a teacher from another room to work in this classroom for a few hours each day, both to add a pair of fresh eyes and to provide some objective feedback. Lori, who'd never worked with toddlers before, left the preschool room and spent each morning in the family room. She played, interacted, and, most importantly, observed the rhythms of the children. Lori commented:

Those rhythms screamed at me: "LET ME PLAY!" So after some discussion and reflection with the teachers, we changed the routine. Rather than separate, distinct transitions for tidying up/snack/small group time/outdoors, it's now *play* right up until outdoor time, with tidying up happening just before they put on their coats. Snack is now open in that children come to eat when they're ready, and small-group times happen during play. Diapering and toilet routines happen as needed rather than interrupting the children. It's a bit of a change for the teachers, because they have to gauge from the children's interest levels when activities need to be switched. It's extremely responsive, and, now that this is being implemented, the routine just flows.

Since she hadn't worked with this age group before, what surprised Lori most was how tremendously capable the toddlers were.

We tried to harness that competence by providing play zones—each with a teacher to observe and then provision the environment—that challenged the children. Perhaps they were bored before, and their behavior was a way of telling us. We had to respond to that.

What Are They Learning?

Toddlers' developmental task includes a tremendous learning curve in terms of language and social/emotional development. At the same time that the teachers in this example were learning to reexamine routines, the toddlers were also learning:

- **Self-direction**. Making their own decisions and choices, leading to increased self-esteem and confidence.

- **Independence**. Taking care of their own needs.

- **Social competence**. How to function and interact, with both children and adults, as a member of a group.

- **Trust**. Understanding that their needs can be expressed and will be met.

The toddler staff had now received input both from an observer who had watched from outside the situation and from someone who had joined them in the day-to-day events of the room and experienced the toddlers' reactions firsthand. It isn't easy to welcome someone into your classroom for the purposes of effecting change, and, as we discussed previously, it takes a particular disposition on the part of the teacher to welcome such disequilibrium. So how did Ali, at that time the lead teacher for this group, feel about the changes?

Mostly, the children seem less confused. Before, we offered a lot of explanations about why we had to tidy up or change activities. But these children are so young.

They just couldn't understand this, and so they became resistant and slow to change activities, and there were a lot of negative behaviors. Now they seem calm and less confused. There's more for them to do in terms of activities, but they can choose whether or not to come to them. And the open snack works well; we tell them when we're about to put the food away just in case they haven't yet thought about eating. Since they are fast-growing toddlers, it's rare that someone doesn't come to eat!

At this point, Ali's disposition was one of openness to change. For the sake of an improved program for the children and a smoother day for the staff, she was willing to undergo a transformation in terms of routine. Although change can be difficult—often more so for adults than for children—professionals realize that it can sometimes be best for everyone. Lisa, too, noticed a change and reported:

Before Lori began offering her support in the toddler room, there was a period when staff members were visibly frustrated with the way they were (or were not, in many cases) following through with observations of the children within their classroom. But once they adopted a responsive approach to the setup of the environment and the activities being offered and reexamined the use of time and routines, the changes were amazing. The children were engaged and interested in what was going on, the teachers were excited about what they were seeing in terms of the children's engagement and exploration, and the negative behaviors disappeared. It's like a different group of children, a different room. We desperately needed this change.

In this chapter, we have seen that there are times, for both new and seasoned teachers, when it's useful to step away from old scripts and ask ourselves:

- Where did this way of doing things originate? Is this the best way for this particular group of children? Why or why not?

- What kind of routine does this group of children need? They are spending a huge part of their lives with us—what are their rights within the flow of the day?

- Are the time spans within the classroom providing for long periods of play, messing about with materials, relaxation and daydreaming, problem solving and decision making? Or does the day instead feel regimented?

- If you were a child in this classroom day after day, how would you feel about the time you spend here? Would you start each day with apprehension, or with delight?

When as teachers we take the important step of thinking critically about our own program or teaching, we open the door to the possibility of a more reflective teaching practice—one that will benefit not only children as the program becomes responsive to them but also teachers as they feel intellectual growth taking place. As we read teachers' stories of this growth in the next chapter, we will see what reflective practice really means—and what it looks like—in their everyday work with children.

Suggested Readings

Reynolds, G., and E. Jones. 1997. *Master Players: Learning from Children at Play*. New York: Teachers College Press.

Wien, C. A. 1995. *Developmentally Appropriate Practice in "Real Life": Stories of Teacher Practical Knowledge*. New York: Teachers College Press.

Untiming the Curriculum: A Case Study of Removing Clocks from the Program

Carol Anne Wien and Susan Kirby-Smith

Author's note: This article was previously published in *Young Children* in September 1998. Some minor changes have been made for inclusion in this book.

Our experiment— Eliminating the production schedule

Tanya and Elizabeth were teachers of a group of eight toddlers 18 to 30 months of age. When they began working together, the morning routine included free play (about 30 minutes), circle, small group, snack, outdoor time, story, and lunch. The pace was rushed, with the teachers trying to keep things "on time," and there were lots of transitions. Though these teachers were skilled and able to keep the routine smooth with little waiting

time, free play (the portion Tanya and Elizabeth agreed was most important) was disappearing due to time constraints.

They had inherited this time schedule from the previous teachers working in this classroom and had taken this schedule for granted as the way things were done, even though no one—certainly not the director or previous teachers—had actually *told* them this. Rather, the toddler teachers had simply absorbed this use of time from living it as they began work in the setting. Since they were new to the center, they deferred to the practice already present. Tanya and Elizabeth were adopting taken-for-granted scripts for organizing time.

At the time, Kirby-Smith was reading Wien's book and was struck by the following quote: "Oddly, the only way I know to break this dominance of time or-

ganization is to focus attention on the organization of space, to make changes in the environment and watch children's responses, and, in the process, to *let time go*, let it vary rather than holding it constant" (Wien 1995, 136). Kirby-Smith wondered how "letting time go" could change practice. What if formal measurement of time—via timepieces—was removed from the classroom? As director, Kirby-Smith invited Elizabeth and Tanya to remove clocks and watches from their classroom, to keep a journal of the impact of this on themselves and the children, and to focus attention on children's interests and needs in making decisions about program and routine. Our report here follows the first 10 months of this process.

A few fixed events and a sequence of events, but beyond that . . .

The plan was simple: the staff would not wear watches, the room would have no clock. The *order* of events would remain unchanged for the children's sense of security. However, the *timing* of changes in activity would be decided according to cues from the children, gathered from teachers' observations. To prepare, the staff reviewed play rhythms in young children, such as Garvey's peaks and valleys (1977) and Montessori's false fatigue ([1949] 1969), in order not to end play prematurely due to misinterpretations of children's engagement.

The basic frame for the day included some immovable parts—staff needed lunch breaks, nap was necessary, arrival and departure times set—and this came to be considered the routine. Everything that was centered around the children and planned by the staff—such as circle, small group, outdoor activity—was considered program. With the clock gone, staff took lunch breaks "whenever the children settled for nap," and lunch was served to the children "whenever they were hungry." Snack was "open" and available during much of the playtime.

At first the teachers were frustrated

What happened for Tanya and Elizabeth when they removed clocks and watches from the room? In the first weeks, the formal program disintegrated. They became so focused on what the children were doing that other components of the day simply did not occur. Circle disappeared because the children were focused on their play. The staff did not want to interrupt the children for small group. Outdoor play some-

times did not occur until the afternoon. The staff complained of "feeling adrift" and feeling that "nothing was happening." And one teacher was so focused on the children's play that the other felt compelled to complete all routine chores—housekeeping, diapers, handwashing, and so forth. She did not appreciate this change in responsibilities!

The children, however, were

> The "schedule," determined by the "clock," often interrupts productive play and intrudes upon young children's natural, creative busynesses. This creates unnecessary transitions and stress.

very happy. Their play was frequently extended for most of the morning and showed teachers new talents and interests. Mark, for example, a quiet and undemanding child 26 months of age, was noticed one day sorting vehicles. To the teachers' astonishment, he made two groups—vehicles that fly and vehicles that don't. The teachers extended his classification at circle, inviting children to choose a vehicle and pretend to move as it moves—quickly, slowly, high, low.

As time went on the teachers became increasingly alert to the children's activity and thinking, and the "rushed" feeling in the classroom was gone. However, another tension took its place. The

two teachers often disagreed in their interpretations of the children's needs and interests. They discovered they had to renegotiate how to make decisions about when to switch to another activity; previously, the clock had decided for them.

One August day, for instance, they were out walking with the children, a casual walk around the neighborhood with talk about what they could see. The children had lots to say and moved slowly, examining each new item encountered—a squished caterpillar, a familiar cat hiding under a porch. Two children new to the program were not used to walking and quickly became fatigued. One teacher thought they should all return to the center. The other noted that the other children were deeply engrossed and had only been out half an hour after a long, rainy week indoors. They were at odds about what to do. Both had the children's interests at heart, but they prioritized needs differently.

For some time the teachers could not agree. Then the idea emerged that one could take the two new children back indoors and the other could take the remaining children to the enclosed center

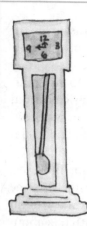

playground where she could safely monitor them. It was the first time it occurred to them they could best serve the divergent needs of the group by splitting up, one going indoors and one staying out. In other words, they found themselves imagining and doing quite different things than ever before. Removing the timepiece as the decisionmaker for when to change activities allowed them to break open the old script for going outside and to imagine new possibilities.

But then things became better than ever

Tanya and Elizabeth's distress concerning how to make decisions based on the children's needs and interests led them, after several weeks, to reexamine what they thought toddlers really needed in a program. After what at times were heated discussions, they reached a consensus on an appropriate program structure for *this particular group* of toddlers. The children needed to be greeted on arrival and helped to make a choice of activity ("planning"), and they required a long period of free play—with snack and toileting taking place naturally within this period but not interrupting the play. A short circle time was to remain because the children so

enjoyed the music and action, and then some outdoor time would follow. Small-group time would move to after the afternoon nap. This plan reduced the number of transitions significantly, and since there were no watches, no particular times were allotted to these components.

Rethinking snacktime

With the clock removed and play frequently continuing throughout the morning, the teachers experimented with inviting the children to tell them when they were hungry, rather than stopping play and imposing a transition to snack. The food would be offered initial-

> When old scripted patterns were broken open and different ways to live events were tried out, new discoveries about the children became possible.

ly to one or two hungry children. Then two things tended to happen: (1) sometimes, when the first children were finished eating, the teachers would casually comment that snack was available if needed; or (2) if the children that day were younger (many of the children were part-time, so ages each day

tended to vary), a crowd of them would eat at the same time, since they found it difficult to wait.

One day several children asked Tanya for something to eat. She brought out oranges, pears, and bananas, knives, napkins, and a plate. Four toddlers gathered around her at a small table. Each child was provided with a plastic knife, and with Tanya's support they began to cut and peel the fruit. This took considerable time—time for sampling, talking, learning to handle the knives, eating as they went. Tanya was unhurried. Snack for these children lasted 20 minutes, and there were more to feed, but there was no sense of hurry. Snack would last as long as it lasted. Elizabeth, across the room, supervised hand washing and toileting and brought other children to snack as the first ones finished. In all, snack lasted 45 minutes because the preparation and eating were so relaxed and full of interest to the children. By the time these children went outside to the playground, the older children were coming inside for lunch. The staff, to their surprise, found that without clocks, this younger age group tended to

eat lunch later than the older children in the center did. They also ate very well, wasting less food, and they slept well and without fuss after lunch.

When old scripted patterns were broken open and different ways to live events were tried out, new discoveries about the children became possible. Who would have thought toddlers would eat lunch late? And why not, if there has been a long and luscious morning snack?

The script is a trap— escaping the trap

Teachers who value and want to support developmentally appropriate practice are often trapped using scripts that arose long ago out of patterns of *teacher dominion* that are still in place in settings today (Wien 1995). A script for teacher dominion gives the teacher power to control what people do; if the teacher follows a production schedule, the child has little power to alter the time frames set by the clock (Wien 1996). When teachers begin work in a pre-established setting, they must follow the time patterns already in place or they are no help to their colleagues. Nor is it likely that newly hired staff have time to negotiate with their teaching partners in much detail before beginning work. As Tanya said: "I was just so happy to be working here. I was new, and everyone had been here longer. I felt I should just follow them, that this was the right way to do things. But it didn't feel right." But the longer the patterns that don't feel right are lived, day-to-day, the more difficult it becomes to change them.

The toddlers are released from artificial constraints

Once the clock was removed from Tanya and Elizabeth's work patterns, a new curriculum began to emerge. It did not focus on an arbitrary program that the teachers believed was "good" for the children. Rather, the children now began to co-own the curriculum with the teachers. Observations were more astute and precise and more cohesively tied to programming.

Peter, for instance, spent a long stretch one day playing with small blocks. He was attempting, with great difficulty, to build a bridge. Tanya offered words of encouragement and described his actions back to him: "You're trying three blocks now instead of two. Will it work? What kind of block do you think you'll need now?" After much experimentation and a great deal of time, he accomplished his first bridge. Before the removal of the clock, Tanya had been too caught up in carrying out the established routine to find the time to watch carefully and support children in such accomplishments, even though she believed she should be providing this support during children's play.

Creative curriculum emerges

Sometimes the new curriculum that emerged swept through the entire group of children. For several days there was intense interest in babies, for instance, and Madeleine decided that she needed to carry her baby in a backpack. The teachers improvised, emptying Madeleine's own backpack of her supplies and popping the doll into it. Madeleine wore the backpack all day, even to nap, and the following day all of the children were wearing backpacks with doll babies tucked into them. The children insisted the babies accompany them everywhere. When they went on walks outdoors, the teachers provided one of the infant unit's strollers for the "babies in backpacks" who wished to ride instead of be carried. These extra preparations required time and effort by the staff as well as obliviousness to embarrassment while walking down the street with a stroller full of dolls in backpacks.

This curriculum about babies was sustained for over a month, with the backpack phase lasting two weeks. All the children and teachers, for example, brought in their own baby photograph. These were placed at the children's eye level on the wall and were revis-

ited many times, the children seeing new similarities and differences between then and now each time they examined the photos. Gradually the children used the babies at small-group time, dressing them in baby clothes with all their intricate fastenings. This then led to the children dressing themselves and seeing the fastening of their own clothing as an intriguing activity.

Some final thoughts

Time organization is the keystone holding together the arch of everyday events. To remove old patterns of time organization calls everything else that teachers do into question and requires teacher reflection about the taken-for-granted scripts for time that they inherited from their predecessors. Reflection permits teachers to invent new scripts that may be more supportive of their conscious desire to construct developmentally appropriate practice. As Elizabeth said: "I don't find it so nerve-wracking now. I thought we were appropriate before, but we weren't anywhere near as flexible as we could have been. [Now] we are more aware of what to look for, what to discuss." Ten months after removing the clocks, both teachers commented that they feel a new sense of freedom to do what they felt they should have been doing all along.

Garvey, C. 1977. *Play.* Cambrige, Mass.: Harvard University Press.

Montessori, M. 1969. *The Absorbent Mind.* New York: Schocken.

Wien, C.A. 1995. *Developmentally Appropriate Practice in "Real Life": Stories of Teacher Practical Knowledge.* New York: Teachers College Press.

Reflective Practice

As teachers observe and interact with children throughout the day, there is so much to consider that it is easy to take observations at face value. Rather than seeing the underlying intent of the children, we may see only the surface of what's happening. As we observe, however, we can ask ourselves, "What is the child working on?" or "What is she trying to understand?" Such questions help us think about the play from the child's perspective, and to consider what to do next. The following anecdote illustrates what kind of new ideas can occur when we take time to reflect.

Through an observation window, several first-year student teachers are watching a toddler as he plays with a truck. For more than ten minutes, he drives the dump truck around the carpet, up the sides of shelving units, over large hollow blocks, and up the wall, while making appropriate truck sound effects. An early childhood professor who's watching along with the students asks, "What do you think is going on here? What might you do in response to this?" The students immediately offer ideas for provisioning the environment: more trucks, roads on the carpet or a way to make them, and so on. After observing for a few more minutes, one student quietly notes: "You know, I don't think it's about the truck. He's keeping his eyes on the wheels, and he's experimenting with where the truck can go. I think it's more about the wheels and the movement."

This wonderful little moment of keen observation and looking under the surface is a first step toward what we strive for in emergent curriculum: reflective practice. What that involves is taking the time to slow down, think deeply, and engage in dialogue with colleagues in order to uncover the child's intentions, thought processes, and prior knowledge—before moving on to the step of planning a carefully considered response.

In this chapter we'll talk about the "missing middle" of reflection in the observation-reflection-planning-observation cycle. Busy teachers who value child-centered curriculum want to move forward in a way that is efficient and yet responsive. When time is short, it can be tempting to simply react rather than take the time to think further. But as we will see, thought together with dialogue can lead to richer curriculum.

The Missing Middle: Taking Time for Reflection

When teachers see something interesting in their everyday work with children (such as the driving of trucks up the wall), there's a tendency to want to respond instantly. There may be a planning form to complete, one with blank spaces waiting for ideas. Or maybe there is limited time available for planning. In order to feel efficient and on top of things, it's tempting to fill in those blank spaces and get the planning done. But when teachers plan without taking time to reflect, something is missing. I call this the "missing middle."

Teachers make choices all day long. But to make informed choices, it's necessary to pause to make connections between what we have seen and what we will do next. These connections are the heart of reflective practice. Rather than following a pattern of observation leading to response, we can instead strive for a pattern of observation leading to reflection leading to response. Such a pause in the action allows us to make meaning of what we've seen. Dialogue with colleagues and with the children themselves is a good place to start. If you are working alone or with people who do not share your philosophy, you can also find ways to reflect upon your own notes and photographs. Let's look at some examples of how reflection can work for early childhood teachers.

Reflecting with Colleagues

What happens when we enter into discussions with other teachers about what we have seen and heard in the classroom? In a team of three, there will probably be three different responses to what has occurred. By taking the time to listen to one another, teachers have the opportunity to expand their own thinking. Truly listening, however, means putting one's own agenda on hold for the time being. And to do this, teachers must be in the moment, not thinking of their own point of view, but trying to understand someone else's.

When teachers are not used to taking the time to think deeply about the meaning of what they have observed, it will take both time and support for them to slow down.

Here is a sample of journal notes I made as we began our emergent curriculum journey at CFDC and attempted to slow down to think.

> **Today during a team meeting we looked closely at the observations that teachers brought along with them. We tried to find the big ideas and the underlying meanings beneath what the children were doing with materials and in the ways they were engaging with each other—and this was a struggle. Some people were not used to thinking this way, with so much attention to detail taking our time. But we persevered, talked it through, and then when we thought we had a sense of the meaning of the play and the children's thinking (this took about an hour), we asked ourselves "What's next? What would be a provocation or invitation to take this a step further?" Brainstorming together helped—ten heads are better than one. We need to think together in order to consider all the possibilities.**

When teachers reflect with their colleagues, several things may take place. They share their thinking, they engage in complex thinking, they think about their own thinking, and they deal with the practicalities—answering thereby the question of what they are going to do in response.

Using Classroom Journals

A shared journal used by all the classroom teachers not only becomes a record of what's been happening throughout the day but also a form of communication between teachers. Usually, a large notebook is left open on a convenient countertop, and teachers jot notes in it all day long. These notes may include brief anecdotes about play, snippets of interesting conversations, questions to oneself or to other teachers, quick sketches of an interesting construction that was missed by the camera—anything goes. When the team meets to reflect, these jottings become the memory of the past few days. When questions arise within a team meeting, the classroom journal can sometimes reveal a pattern or provide details about the topic.

Sharing Thinking

Over time, by analyzing and interpreting what we are seeing, we begin to form our own theories about what is happening in the classroom. This process can help us become more responsive to children, continue to be learners ourselves, and be more thoughtful teachers.

One of the concrete ways that teachers can show their abstract thinking is to provide a rationale—whether stated in writing through documentation notes, or on a planning sheet, or verbally to each other—for everything they do in the classroom. A rationale describes why we are doing what we're doing, thereby making our own thinking visible and helping us articulate our ideas and reasons to others. Explicitly stating one's rationale is good practice for thinking through why we are using a particular approach or activity in our classrooms. When making a decision in a teaching team, it's always useful to ask each other "Why?" Teachers do this not in order to be contrary but to help one another think through their rationale for everything they plan to do in the classroom. Over time, through practicing this kind of discourse, teachers become very adept at thinking out loud and explaining their reasoning. When teachers are good at this, it engages them intellectually and validates their work. They also experience increased confidence about their reasons for teaching the way they do.

Engaging in Complex Thinking

Complex thinking can be described as holding many theories, perspectives, or ideas in mind at the same time, connecting some of them so that we can make informed choices and creative decisions.

When teachers keep in mind all the aspects of what has been observed in the classroom, and when they think about all the different influences (for example, theories, philosophies, previous experiences) that might affect the situation being examined, they are engaging in complex thinking. Rather than simply saying, for instance, "When this child draws birds over and over again, she is developing fine-motor skills and learning how to represent," we might also consider the representations in other ways: Can we see a particular focus within these drawings? What is it about birds that is so fascinating for this child? What is her prior knowledge? Her misunderstanding? In what other ways can she show us what she knows? How does her thinking link to theories of child development? To artistic and creative development? Do her drawings have connections to other things that she knows about or has experienced? It's not that the first understanding is incorrect, but rather that it is only one valid way of thinking about a child's work. Complex thinking allows teachers to consider a child's work from multiple perspectives at the same time, opening up more possibilities for further action, or perhaps even the realization that further observation is needed before a decision can be made.

Deb Curtis and Margie Carter (2000) suggest examining children's play from three perspectives: the child's story, the learning and development story, and the teacher's story. Perhaps in your training, you were encouraged to constantly look for the learning and development in what engages children. As Curtis and Carter point out, however, it is important to consider all perspectives, including the teacher's point of view, in order to get the big picture. What excites or puzzles or delights you about what you are seeing? When I ask students or teachers to think about their own perspective, I ask, "What do you wonder? What are you curious about? How can you find out more?"

As for considering the children's perspective, you might ask, "Why do these children keep returning to this play? What fascinates them about this particular idea? What are they saying about it? What is their previous experience with this scenario? How many ways can I provide for them to show what they know?"

Thinking about Thinking

Thinking about our own thinking (metacognition) is an exercise in self-awareness and an opportunity for growth, since it can help us to identify our own learning styles and ways of knowing. Thinking about your own thinking, and listening to your team as they do the same, enables you to understand both your own decision-making process within the classroom and the points of view of your colleagues. Do you find yourself constantly approaching curriculum from the same perspective? If so, perhaps there's room for you to grow and experiment in this area. Or perhaps you admire a colleague's ability to see a situation from many angles; can you learn from her? How do you make decisions? The process of considering these questions may lead you to greater self-awareness in your teaching.

Dealing with Practical Issues

The construction of knowledge is a wonderful thing in itself, but it isn't of much practical use if we cannot apply it within our work. Any team of teachers will come up with different meanings for what they've seen and different ways to respond. Handling differences requires that teachers be able to recognize patterns, organize their thinking, make connections, and select responses. Within this selection process, teachers must consider all possibilities, weigh them within the context of what's happening with a particular group of children, and make the best choices they can, using the resources they have.

Teachers commonly bemoan the fact that they do not have enough materials, or money, or time, to do the things they would like to do in their classrooms. What you must remember is that you, as a teacher, are the biggest resource of all. Supporting children as they work and using your creativity in setting up an interesting environment are two of your most important roles. Putting your ideas into practice takes skill, time, and reflection, but being able to do this is what makes wonderful things happen in an early childhood program.

Finding Time for Reflection

Considering all the questions raised above and the need to consider many options and perspectives, the process of reflection may appear to be very time consuming. How does the process of reflection fit into a busy day in an early childhood setting? This kind of thinking certainly takes time. Ideally, teachers would have an hour or more a week for dialogue with their colleagues. Some centers provide out-of-classroom planning or reflection time for their teachers. Providing substitutes or other coverage to make this happen is usually difficult, however, and many directors simply cannot provide it. Other centers require that teachers meet after work on a regular basis, or encourage teams to think together during children's naptimes rather than giving precedence to more routine tasks. Again, not everyone has this kind of time or support built into their work lives. Here are some other ways that teachers build reflective practice into their daily work:

- **Take many digital photographs**. If you cannot find the time yourself, have someone else take photos of the children while they're engaged in play. Rather than waiting for a "perfect photo" or "cute" photo opportunities, focus instead on children working intently with materials, rearranging the environment, negotiating with peers, engaged in solitary play, and so on. Later, as you review the photographs, you are likely to find two or three that intrigue you. What exactly is it that fascinates you about what's going on? What is unexpected or puzzling? Delightful? Is there something going on here that makes you want to know more? That makes you wonder? Share the photographs with your team (you don't need a meeting to do this, it can be quite informal) and with the children themselves. What do they have to say about the photographs? Children can be extremely articulate about their own work and love to talk about what they were thinking at the time. Early morning, late in the day, or as they awake from nap are good times to revisit their work with them; these times allow for quiet conversations (switch on a tape recorder if you have one, or take notes).

- **Set aside staff meeting time for discussion of children's work**. At Emerson Preschool, a majority of the time at every weekly staff meeting is set aside for discussion of children's work. Teachers share written anecdotes and pore over photographs and samples of children's representations. Their questions about what the children are doing help the teachers to think together, thus deepening and enlivening their discussion. Teachers try to concentrate on uncovering children's thinking and intentions, as well as the connections they are making between their life experiences and their play.

- **Create documentation panels**. During naptime, or at home if that works for you, make small documentation panels to post outside your classroom for other teachers and parents to see. Be sure to provide a place for writing down questions or thoughts they have. If there's no time for dialogue, seeing other people's questions in writing may help you think in new ways.

Sustaining Reflective Practice

If you have the desire to think about ideas and discuss them with others, you will need to seek out like-minded people to think and talk with on a regular basis. Tossing ideas around is appealing to most teachers, and along with this brainstorming, sharing, and playful interaction come new and creative ways to think about what children are doing and to find meaning in their work that may otherwise go undiscovered.

There are some concrete, practical things you can do in order to engage other teachers in discussion and reflection. These include creating a discussion group, finding a mentor or peer coach, using technology to connect long-distance, and journaling.

Create a Group Outside Work

If no time can be allotted at your workplace for discussions and thinking together, or if you work alone, or if you have no colleagues who are interested in exploring emergent curriculum with you, consider joining (or starting!) a group outside of work.

Here's how one emergent curriculum collaborative was started. In 2007, a group of educators in Concord, a small city in New Hampshire, realized that they needed time to talk together. All of them had either been using an emergent curriculum approach for some time or were just beginning to investigate this way of responding to children. There were also some students who were studying and practicing this approach in practicum settings and needed dialogue with more experienced peers in order to grow.

As their practicum coordinator, I was able to bring the students, their cooperating teachers, and other interested individuals (such as professors and directors) together for monthly discussions. These were informal, supportive, and conversational in tone. The goal was to support one another through a process of thinking together and engaging in dialogue about curriculum. Each time we met, two or three individuals would share their work. It is important to note that they shared not only their successes but also their struggles. Many had burning questions. Rather than attempting to fully answer questions, we instead offered ideas for gathering more information, thinking in new ways, or trying alternate approaches.

Rena, for instance, brought to the group stories of children's fascination with auto racing. She knew that the families of many children in her class were avid racing fans who took their children with them to races nearby. The children in her group, all five-year-olds, had a sophisticated vocabulary for this topic, knew the names of famous drivers and their numbers, and watched racing on TV. Seeing children interested in building cars, Rena wanted to offer opportunities for this. The group suggested that she provide very open-ended materials. But everyone present also wanted to discuss this topic at a deeper level. What is it about speed and racing that engages children? How does parent involvement in a hobby or sport influence children? What would be some in-depth ways of scaffolding children's already extensive knowledge on the topic, and could parents be involved with this? Rather than going away with lists of things to do, Rena left with many more questions to ponder, as well as things to watch for and find out about. She was quite happy with this, and later reported that she felt challenged, which she found was a positive thing.

Find a Mentor

A mentor is someone who advises, nurtures, models, and helps you to move forward. Finding someone like this provides a huge opportunity for personal growth.

Perhaps there's someone in your community, or even within your own organization, whose work you admire. Sometimes we discover such a person through attending conferences or workshops or in more serendipitous ways. If you strike up a conversation with a professional and feel a connection with their philosophy, ideas, or approaches, stay in touch with that person! If the person is local, ask if you might get together once a month, perhaps over coffee or at one of your centers, to talk about ideas, and share experiences. Corresponding via e-mail is an option for busy professionals who don't live close to each other. The following message was sent to me by a former student who now teaches preschool children full time. I mentored her for several years, but since I've moved away from her area, we keep in touch by e-mail:

> **Hi, Susan. I just wanted to let you know that I've changed jobs. I couldn't do what they wanted me to do in the classroom because it just didn't feel right to me. I was getting so frustrated. But you always told me to try to find a "good fit" and now I've found one! I'm working at a different center, and the lead teacher I'm working with is awesome. We're on the same page, and I feel really comfortable with her. I'm so glad I made the change, and I'll keep you posted.**

This teacher, remembering something she learned in college (finding a good fit), chose to keep in touch with me about her career change because she knows that I care and will offer encouragement, even though I'm far away. You probably know someone who has given you good advice over the years, acted as your sounding board, and encouraged you to try new things (or else to step back and take a deep breath!). Mentors are important to us; professionals need a sounding board in order to think through important life and career changes. Sometimes mentors can help us see things more clearly, and sometimes just being able to talk things through helps us make our own decisions.

Look for a Peer Coach

Is there a teacher in another classroom who likes to explore ideas and talk about his work, someone you find easy to talk with? If so, here's a chance to partner with someone and chat informally at lunchtime or before or after work. Such a person can be a listener and a coach for your ideas. And since he's not in your classroom, he can provide additional perspective through his feedback. Or perhaps there's someone within your own team whom you can chat with informally throughout the day. This can feel like not working, but as Liz Rogers, a seasoned teacher in Burlington, Vermont, explains, such teacher talk can be extremely valuable to your classroom.

> Our vision as a staff is to share our teaching journey both on and off the floor. We exchange stories at staff meetings and planning times but also among the children and families of our community every day. Although we have been valuing one another's unique and insightful contributions in meetings outside the classroom for many years, we noticed that as a team of teachers we weren't availing ourselves of one another's viewpoints and expertise while in the classroom.

> We wanted to do something about our tendency to teach alone, to rely solely on our own skills and knowledge. So we agreed to make an intentional effort to talk more while we were working. In some ways, this endeavor was easy: asking a coteacher about his weekend, sharing a story about a play scenario, delighting in a child's clay work over a cup of coffee, or offering to jot down notes for a coteacher who's engaged with a group of children. It also meant taking an interest in each others' passions, encouraging one another to share these parts of our life at school.

> For example, through our conversations, Siobhan's interest in theater and dance led her to offer dance classes on Saturday mornings. Although technically this class extends beyond our regular work hours and includes children beyond those enrolled in our program, it contributes to our community on several levels. Parents enjoy coffee and conversation while the children dance. New and enrolling children have a chance to connect with and explore the center, claiming a sense of place for themselves so that when they arrive at our program they already have the feeling of belonging and their transition is eased. The dance class is meaningful for both Siobhan and the children who are realizing and sharing her passion.

> Lengthy conversations among coteachers about our shared value of developing the feeling of home at school encouraged another of my coteachers, Jason, to share his love of carpentry by bringing our idea of a kitchen table to life. Teachers wanted a comfortable, familiar place to sit with the community, and Jason built the table along with the children. It's been the center of a beloved place in our school for many years now.

> We're learning that choosing to talk while we teach is complex, requiring ongoing practice and thoughtful risk taking. Breaking the habit of doing

everything on my own in order to feel like a successful and competent teacher calls for hard personal work. Asking for help when I need it, even though it makes me feel vulnerable, is challenging. So is figuring out how not to talk too much, and knowing when not to add my two cents. I need to be in tune with my coteachers so that we balance well together. It takes ongoing thoughtful practice not to feel confronted or not to confront others with help. Rather, we need to support and be present for one another.

It takes effort to develop our abilities to listen to one another, understanding that each teacher's perspective, even when it conflicts with our own, says something about our shared work among the children. Exercising both our listening and our unique voices ensures that we teach in a connected rather than a disconnected way. Entering into and negotiating partnership during curriculum planning and project work fundamentally changes our individual teaching by including others and being affected by the meaning making that grows from shared experiences. Giving ourselves permission to talk, teacher to teacher, throughout the early childhood program day is an important step in teaching and in learning collaboratively as a staff.

By welcoming dialogue, we choose to exercise our ability to actively listen to one another as well as to strengthen cooperative skills in our daily teaching. Allowing ourselves to talk intentionally generates opportunities to partner with the community, where individual ventures (activities and projects) between a teacher and a group of children often open up to more integrated and resourceful learning experiences for all.

Welcoming teacher talk in the classroom frees each of us from feeling guilty about our human need and desire to connect and converse with one another as adults and as educators. Intently valuing each other's company while working with the children makes our relationship, our connectedness, and our joy and support for each other visible to the children and families and, even more important, encourages our playfulness.

Through conversations in the classroom, Liz and her colleagues have learned to value one another's perspectives, to teach together instead of individually, and to use their shared experiences to build curriculum. It is clear that there is a strong sense of community in this classroom, one that leads to trusting in each other and delighting in each other's work.

Use Technology

If you are working alone or in a situation where others don't share your enthusiasm for exploring new approaches, technology can help you connect with like-minded professionals—not only in your community, but across the country and around the world. With some minor searching, you can find links to discussion lists, online journals with discussion boards, places to post your own work/projects, and so on. If you're fairly confident with technology, you can start your own blog. Sites such as blogger.com or livejournal.com are easy to join and cost nothing. These sites provide an opportunity to both share your work and discuss it with parents, students, and other interested parties. Access to a blog can be controlled by the blog manager (you!), and blogging can take as much or as little time as you choose to invest.

When researching online groups and journals, it's worth taking the time to find something that really fits with your philosophy and your developmental stage as a teacher, as well as to ensure that the site is indeed professional and reputable. You may also find an online journal such as the Co-Inquiry Journal (www.coinquiry.org) extremely useful, since it deals with reflective practice and includes in-depth discussions of investigations.

Keep a Journal

Another way of reflecting on what's happening in your classroom is to keep a journal. People have been writing their thoughts in journals for hundreds of years. A journal can be private or shared, but it is always thought provoking. When we read entries from our past, journals show us our own growth. Sometimes, the simple act of writing down our thoughts helps us to think more clearly. For this reason, many early childhood programs ask student teachers to write journal entries on a regular basis. Though the approaches toward and purposes of journal entries differ from school to school, they all have a common goal: to develop reflective practitioners. The following example is from the journal of a student teacher. Tereza is a mature student who has already worked with young children for several years while taking evening classes at the same time. This reflection was written in response to a math assignment from a curriculum class that was carried out in her classroom.

> **The idea that math is fun and can be learned through daily activities is a new concept for me. During my own early childhood, math was something to be memorized, and the only way to learn it was through worksheets. I realize that learning math has become easier, in part due to the use of open-ended manipulative materials. As a result, mathematical concepts such as number recognition, shapes, counting, and patterns don't have to be memorized; they are experienced. Even though I've learned that math can become more of a hands-on subject, I believe that I've underestimated children's abilities to explore math. My expectations as a teacher used to be that if a child aged five or six was able to count by rote and recognize numbers, and if they had some problem-solving skills, they'd attained the "necessary skills."**

Math Conversation Assignment

Children express their ideas in many "languages," including how they use materials and what they say about what they're doing with them.

In this assignment, students in a curriculum class were asked to observe children during play in several areas of the classroom, paying particular attention to any math concepts that naturally arose. When possible, the students were to enter into conversation with the children about what they were doing, trying to understand their thinking through authentic conversations, with a focus on listening rather than questioning.

After the conversation, students were asked to reflect on what had been said, and respond to what they'd learned about the child's math understanding by planning an invitation or activity. This could be a small- or large-group activity, or for an individual child.

Included in the students' assignment was the requirement for a rationale for the activity they had provided.

But, as I've been exposed to more information and critical thinking, my views on how children construct their mathematical knowledge have changed. I now realize that children build their knowledge by experimentation with the environment, exploration of materials, interaction with adults and other children, and their own observations. As I read my textbook and articles, and undertook my math activity and conversation assignment, I was able to better understand some of the developmental practices in teaching math. One example would be the use of calendar routines with young children. I always assumed that just because I've seen it used in each classroom, it would be something normal and appropriate. It never occurred to me that young children can't completely understand abstract concepts such as time. I realize now that I can make use of calendar routines if I take into consideration the children's development and make it more personal to the child's point of view. I need to find ways for time to be meaningful to children, or else not use this activity. Another aspect I've learned in teaching math has been the importance to listen, observe, and interact with children. The math conversation activity has showed me how valuable observations can be in becoming a more effective teacher.

I do believe that as a teacher I'm always learning from the children. I realize that each year I'm trying something new. This may be the result of my observations of children's interactions with materials, or my own experimentation with things that work or don't work. This process is important because it empowers me to make changes not only as a teacher but also as a learner. I also realize that the readings have affected the way I think about math and helped me with new ideas and a fresh approach. As a result, I plan to continue using math in daily activities, as part of classroom routines, transitions, and daily conversations, and to make use of observations to determine children's understanding of mathematical concepts.

In her response, Tereza reflected not only on her prior knowledge and childhood experiences but also on her own learning from classes, readings, and assignments. And she also examined the shifts she has made in her thinking about, and approaches to, teaching math. Besides thinking about what changed, however, she also considers how this change, or her "aha" moment, came about. Tereza examines, in her reflection on calendar routines, what led her to do this activity in the first place, the information she was exposed to that changed her thinking, and how she might approach this in the future. This is what Carol Ann Wien calls a "pivot point" (Wien 1995, 53). Such a moment is typical of reflective practice—a teacher recognizes a struggle, a puzzle, or something that doesn't work, and thinks deeply about the struggle until a new approach becomes clear.

Teacher Development and Reflective Practice

As we have seen, reflective teachers develop not in a vacuum but in situations where they feel supported and are able to talk through their struggles with others of like mind, situations where their careful consideration of children's actions is valued. Developing the habit of thinking reflectively, considering all perspectives, and thereby reaching moments of enlightenment or creativity does not happen overnight, or in isolation.

The teachers and students I have worked with have experienced a series of predictable stages in order to reach a comfort level with reflective practice, but the levels of support they have needed throughout these stages have differed. Generally, new teachers or those new to emergent practices begin with quite concrete observations of what children are doing with materials and with each other. At this stage, teachers are often unsure of exactly what they are looking for, so they focus on what is immediately apparent. The trouble with this approach is that there is so much to respond to when observing in a busy early childhood environment.

Over time, the teacher learns to refine observations by listening to children's conversations, thinking about their thinking, and trying to respond to both their thinking and their actions. At this stage, observations tend to become more abstract as the teacher begins to make connections between what has been done before, what has been said, and children's prior knowledge. Sometimes, if the teacher is experienced, she may compare present situations with her prior experiences, and she may be able to draw upon her repertoire of skills and responses. As a teacher develops into reflective practice, she may, through dialogue or further education, be able to reach some understanding of the children's underlying intent. The more seasoned we become, the more willing we are to form hypotheses—that is, to make an educated guess about what's happening for the child and what we may be able to do about that.

Once we have spent some time in this kind of practice, it's less intimidating to find out that we were quite wrong about something and to take a step back in order to reassess. We begin to see this as a learning experience, and to grow from it. Finally, reflective teachers are able to create—from their questions and their data collection through observation—the role of researcher, a role discussed in chapter 7.

But at this point, what kinds of support will this teacher need in order to reach her full potential? In many centers, the director takes on the role of supporter, mentor, facilitator, and coach. For those fortunate enough to employ a program coordinator or consultant, that person can work with reflective teachers in the role of provocateur or mentor. Whoever this person is, she must be attuned to individual learning styles, the stage of each teacher in her journey, and the resources available to the organization. As she follows the staff through their journeys, she becomes part cheerleader and part coach, matching her support to their needs. Different teams will, of course, need different kinds of encouragement. But some needs are common: the need for time to talk, for materials for documentation, for support in decision making when teachers are new to the process, and for validation of the work that teachers are doing.

The accompanying chart describes the work done with CFDC teachers as they emerged into reflective practice. This is a very specific example, so you may not be able to use all the same approaches. For instance, you'll see that at one point I used videotape, which may not be available to you. Instead, you could take notes and photographs the staff could use during discussion at a later date.

Reading from side to side and from column to column, one can see that for each stage of teacher growth, there's a response in the form of a supporting role.

Reflective Practice: A Process of Growth as Experienced at NHTI Child and Family Development Center	
Teacher's Growth	**Supporting Role (Director)**
(Beginning from the recognition that curriculum comes from the children)	(Beginning with the idea of teacher as researcher needing support)
Basic concrete observations relating mostly to how children use things, but also to their development.	Reminder of three perspectives as outlined by Curtis and Carter. Questions: What is the big picture? How can you widen the lens? What do you wonder? Change of notetaking format.
Observations of process and people; beginning to notice children's thinking and connections they've made. Thinking is shifting to slightly more abstract.	Random videotaping in classrooms to help staff slow down and see the bigger picture, the context, have time to think about this. Questions: Can you name the play? What's the plot?
Observing for, then naming the play, and making educated inferences (Jones and Reynolds 1992).	Remove the pressures in terms of writing the plan, and create time for talk. Question: Which theorist does this observation remind you of?
Observing, having time to reflect and talk, telling stories, trying to get at children's reasoning. Shift in focus of documentation panels; now trying to make thinking visible.	Continue videotaping, sitting in on meetings in order to hold onto teachers' thoughts for them and acting as scribe.
Evolving Role: Teacher as Researcher	Evolving Role: Director as Provocateur

The Teacher's Voice: "Aha" Moments and Turning Points

Asking other teachers to think together has been a valuable experience for some teachers in Concord's Emergent Curriculum Collaborative. Here, we look at what happened when Lori's team was perplexed, and also somewhat irritated, by a persistent play idea: puppies.

For some reason, children love to act out being baby animals—particularly puppies and kittens. Complete with meowing and yipping, crawling around the floor, leashes, kennels, and pet beds, it's a recurring play theme in early childhood settings. In the preschool room at CFDC, the teachers watched as this play idea came up once more. Most of the children in the group were involved, and the classroom was filled with the sounds of children yipping and howling as they crawled about and took care of their "pets." In discussing the play with other teachers, Lori expressed her concerns. She wanted to support the children's play, but she also saw that they were using no recognizable language for days at a time, and she worried about that. In addition, the classroom felt chaotic to all the teachers. Here, in Lori's words, is what happened.

Technically, this subject began as puppy play. We teachers recognized our frustrations surrounding puppy play: it made the classroom feel chaotic, and rather than being very complex play, it seemed to be simplistic and repetitive. Yet at the same time, because of its recurring nature and the children's deep engagement, we realized that it was important to the children

In searching for direction, we decided to take the issue to the Emergent Curriculum Collaborative for discussion among colleagues who weren't in the thick of it. As a team, we truly were *not* seeking curriculum ideas surrounding dogs. Rather than discouraging the children's play, we were looking for the deeper meaning behind the question "Why puppies?"

After I explained the team's feelings about this play, we received the following responses/thoughts from the group:

- What is the role of dramatic play? Do we allow all kinds of dramatic play, or limit them?

- Do dogs have a language? Are the children communicating?

- Perhaps children should be encouraged to tell their dog stories.

- Perhaps puppy play brings out nurturance in children.

- The teachers' irritation is real—don't ignore it. Perhaps the team could think about where it stems from. Does time of day have anything to do with this? Does the irritation come from feeling a lack of control over the environment?

- Perhaps journaling could help. Does the play change? At what point do the feelings of irritation arise?

- What is the role of dogs in society? In our culture? Does being a dog allow the child to be passive? Active? Avoid responsibility?

- Loudness is contagious and becomes hard to manage. Rather than disregarding the situation, examine it.

The group reflection process generated lots of thoughts and even more questions. I was a little overwhelmed—like my brain was full! But, I was also rejuvenated, for through their responses our colleagues had provided a thread to follow in our quest for answers.

In this example, we can see how both thinking together and the questions generated by the larger group gave the team more to consider and an opportunity to examine the situation from different perspectives. In chapter 5, we will see how the team responded following their reflection process.

When thinking about discussing one's work with others, Lori says:

I think each team needs a provocateur—someone, or a group of people, willing to encourage the team to take a risk with their thinking, to offer a new perspective, and then encourage the teachers to move ahead. Team members need to feel validated.

If there's a team leader, then the leader must be willing to let go of her ego and allow each teacher the opportunity to feel ownership, a sense of purpose, and success.

The term *provocateur* is not commonly used in reference to early childhood education or educators. If, however, we think of a provocation as something that arouses a response, then the kind of provocateur Lori is referring to can push you further in your thinking. Someone can do this by asking interesting questions that make you think harder, or think in a different way. Or a person may disagree with you, therefore encouraging a lively discussion. Sometimes a provocateur may offer her own thoughts on something, and you might choose to disagree. Discussions (and argument!) are good tools for thinking harder and for thinking beyond our usual limits. They can generate very creative ideas and "aha" moments that make us feel enlightened by a new thought or excited about trying a new approach.

A provocateur could be your director, a fellow teacher, a professor, or some other mentor. If you have someone in your life who loves to discuss or argue about ideas with you, this could be your provocateur. Value this person. She or he may take your thinking to higher levels.

The Child's Voice: Slowing Down

To be reflective, teachers need to reflect not only upon their own practice but also upon children's ideas. Sometimes these are easy to miss, or to dismiss. If we take a few moments to consider and try to understand children's ideas, surprising things can happen.

In a class of three- to five-year-olds at Purdue University's Lab School, teachers observed as several children became fascinated with birds. They used binoculars at the large windows to watch the wide variety of species that inhabited the bare winter trees in their playground. The children had many questions and a lasting interest. So the teachers collaborated with them in an in-depth study of birds. They invited experts from the university campus to share their knowledge and offered resources for children to do research of their own. All of this was proceeding well and the children were very engaged, when one child's actions dramatically changed the course of the project. And it almost went unnoticed.

During play, five-year-old Liam found a ball of string in the studio area and invited a student teacher to come to the outer cubby room. Once there, he asked the student to help him attach one end of the string high up on the wall. Although happy to oblige, the student was unclear about what was going on in Liam's mind. When she asked him "What for?" he wasn't yet able to articulate his idea. The student went ahead and attached the string, and then Liam asked her to continue attaching the ever-growing length of string around the room. Other children, of course, became intrigued by this, and so did the teachers.

> I was the lead teacher in this room at the time, and after watching awhile, I had a conversation with Liam. Instead of asking him what he was doing, I instead tried "What are you thinking about?" in order to understand what he had in mind. Liam responded, "It's a flight path."

> After the children had left, the teaching staff in the room met briefly to reflect on what would happen next. We realized that we needed to know more about Liam's thinking and his prior experiences. How does a five-year-old know about flight paths? Did he have a particular interest in airplanes? And what about the other children? They were certainly interested in weaving string around the room. Was that the only thing that was interesting to them, or did they understand something about what Liam was doing? Rather than rush in with plans for the next day, we decided to first approach Liam's parents, and then observe further before making any decisions.

> When we spoke with Liam's father the next day, he explained that Liam had often flown around the country with his parents, and when he got bored they often perused the onboard flight magazines together. The pages at the back of those magazines illustrate the airline's flight paths around the world. Following those paths to see where they led, had become a familiar experience for Liam. Aha!

Even though we'd solved the mystery of Liam's prior knowledge, we still didn't change the environment or plan activities. For several days, we watched and talked as a team about how the other children were becoming involved. Many children were now winding string around the room, until it looked like a giant spiderweb. A small group of children had incorporated their interest in birds by making paper birds they could attach to the strings and pull around the room on their flight paths. Others began discussing what was needed in order to fly. Hearing the children's theories about this—including many misunderstandings—and after engaging in further dialogue, the teaching staff now had enough information to settle on a plan. We decided to switch gears slightly in order to concentrate more on the process of flight than on birds, and to provocations such as opportunities to make flying machines, explore the effect of wind using a fan, and so on. Thus, the flight project was born.

Looking back on this project, we realized that it would have been easy to continue with our investigation of birds. But Liam's small action, the fact that he was allowed to wind string around the room at a height of about four feet (which meant many entanglements for adults), and the other children's engagement in all of this allowed us to reexamine our direction. His actions were thought provoking for the other children, and they facilitated the teachers' thinking in a new direction. Had he not been allowed to demonstrate the connections between his own experiences and our classroom work, and if the teachers hadn't taken the time to reflect on his ideas and ask questions, the flight project and all the learning that went with it would not have happened.

Looking back on the flight project, the teachers later reiterated that the noticing of each child's actions, the responses of the other children, and the discussions among staff were the key factors in the decision-making process around this work.

Now that you are thinking—and perhaps thinking differently—about your possible responses to children's ideas, it is time to make a plan and take action. Rather than describe possible actions in black-and-white terms, the next chapter discusses the possibilities. As with many creative acts, what happens next in any classroom situation depends on what happened before, and how. Therefore, we will take a look at several possibilities for planning next steps.

Suggested Reading

Curtis, D., and M. Carter. 2008. *Learning Together with Young Children: A Curriculum Framework for Reflective Teachers.* St. Paul: Redleaf Press.

5

From Reflection to Curriculum

Imagine that in one week, you and your team have collected a small stack of written anecdotes, a couple of narratives, and several photos of children in action. You also have several examples of children's work: their drawings, plus models and other artifacts. You have taken all of this with you to a team meeting, and you have had some time to think deeply about the play and what it might mean. Now what? It's time to think about what you have seen and understood (or not), and how to respond to that with curriculum. If you have never planned this way, generating curriculum ideas from reflecting on your observations may feel like stepping off a precipice, with no idea where you are going to land. Rather than feeling nervous about this, consider taking the stance that such disequilibrium is a good thing! It prods teachers to think harder, to be more creative, and to collaborate—not only with their teams, but with children.

After reflecting with colleagues, teachers can take several paths in responding to what they've seen and heard:

- They can plan some invitations or a provocation to further explore the children's interest in a topic.

- They can provision the environment with additional materials that support the children's play.

- They can take the children outside of the school environment.

- They can invite an "expert" to visit and talk with the children.

The team will also need to consider how to group the children to pursue the interest they've observed. How many children are interested in the topic or play idea? Only rarely is a whole group fixed on a common interest, but that shouldn't stop teachers from proceeding. What can be investigated with small groups of children? With large groups? With individual children? How we organize groups of children has a huge effect on how curriculum emerges, and so this topic is covered as well.

Finally, this chapter addresses the issue of planning in advance and recording your plans. Writing down the plan is always a challenge when teachers are planning based on their observations of children's play, but it's often necessary so that parents, administrators, licensers, and others can see teachers' thought processes at work. In this chapter, you will see a CFDC work-in-progress and explore some ways of making your curriculum planning work visible.

Provocations and Invitations

Once you have taken the time to observe and reflect, it's time to act on your thinking. After observation and reflection, you will be deciding whether you want to plan a response or if you need to find out more. One way to make that decision is to provide a provocation or a set of invitations for the children and then watch for the response.

A provocation can be described as an action or question likely to produce retaliation. In our society, this word has somewhat negative undertones. But in teaching, we might

think of provocation as "listening closely to the children and devising a means for provoking further thought and action" (Fraser and Gestwicki, 2002, 11). An invitation is a way to test the waters in exploring just how interested the children are, a way of researching which direction to take. An invitation might be an intriguing set of materials that tie into the children's interest, something new in a learning center, a display that invites hands-on exploration, or perhaps library books on the topic.

Carol Anne Wien suggests that a provocation is "something that must be responded to, that we cannot ignore" (C. A. Wien, pers. comm.). An invitation, on the other hand, may or may not be taken up. How you set up the activity/materials delineates whether they are an invitation or a provocation. Inviting materials set up for play might be explored and discussed by the children, or they might be ignored. But a challenge of some sort (within discussion with a teacher, perhaps, or as a problem to be solved through action by the children) is harder to ignore and is more likely to invoke a response.

Offering an invitation or a provocation is one way you can find out more about the children's thinking. How the children respond to the materials will provide teachers with information about what to do next. Whether you are acting alone or with colleagues, your planning will become easier once you have clarified for yourself, through reflection, what it is that the children are working on, and what they are trying to understand.

Consider these examples:

Looking Through

Monica, a student teacher in a toddler classroom at CFDC, notices that all the children are fascinated with looking through objects and materials. They examine almost all of the classroom materials in this way. To explore both their level of interest and exactly what it is about looking through that interests them, she sets out a number of invitations for the children: funnels, cardboard tubes with colored cellophane over the ends, and cameras that no longer work but provide a viewfinder to peer through. She has no particular agenda for how the children might use these materials. Instead, she takes a wait and see stance.

The children show particular interest in the cardboard tubes, and Monica describes how she picked up on this and how they were used for over a week:

> **I taped some tubes together, and also provided larger tubes and different widths of plastic tubing. I'd leave them on a table for when the children woke up, and they always went right to them. But besides looking through them, they also put the tubes to their mouths and ears, experimenting with sounds. This was unexpected. Some of the children stacked the tubes, and this provided a challenge very different from working with blocks. The tubes were played with for over a week before they started to fall apart . . . and now we know that it's possible to explore ways to make different sounds while also providing building materials.**

Playing Bank

In an afterschool classroom in Concord, Jessica—an ECE student studying in the evenings while working during the day—watched as children struggled to make paper money. They did not attempt to make coins. They wanted to play bank. Jessica thought about how to support this, and she also wondered why they weren't interested in coins. As an invitation, she provided some play and real money, including some Canadian coins, as well as withdrawal slips and checks, and stood back to watch.

In her written reflection about the children's responses, Jessica talks about how this play took off beyond her expectations:

> The children really enjoyed their new money. Two weeks later, they continue to be engaged with the bank—it has resulted in a pizza parlor so that they can spend their money! The boy who started the whole bank idea has now learned some organizational skills. He has a box he keeps everything in, has labels for each bank account that the children have opened, and he keeps inventory on the money. He takes his bank very seriously. He told me: "Well actually, I have to take responsibility—seeing how I opened this thing up." The children have learned how to count their money, write checks, and take out loans; all with the help of one another and very little scaffolding from me, except to explain to one child what a withdrawal slip was for—he then connected this to what he'd seen his mother do at the bank. The children even understood that the bank might not accept their Canadian money (which the children thought was "way cool," asking where they could get some).

Such student assignments give educators-in-training the chance to experience what can happen when we add invitations to the environment. We may not have a clear idea of what will unfold, but if we are willing to take the time to slow down and watch the responses, the children will provide us with a direction.

A Provocation in the Block Area

The preschool children at Jubilee Road Children's Center in Halifax had been moving furniture and manipulatives between two large classroom areas in order to play out their ideas about construction workers in the block area. Part of this construction work involved trying to make hoists to lift up various materials. After some reflection, the teaching team decided that the children were stuck in terms of how to make their hoists work better—materials often fell off the end of their rope due to lack of a secure knot, or else the material was too heavy to lift. Deciding to do something provocative, the team surprised the children with a complete change in the block area one morning: a series of pulleys and ropes—with hooks on the end—had been set up. In order to make their ideas about lifting work, the children had to pay attention to this new piece of equipment. The ropes had been taken away. There was no ignoring this change; it was provocative and it had to be responded to.

The children did indeed respond—there was no choice but to use the area differently now that the materials were different. The children were excited when they realized that the materials were easier to combine and lift as the play spread over the larger physical space that the pulleys covered. Their play, though unchanged in terms of the big idea, now became more and more complex, as if the provocation both facilitated deeper thinking about their topic and provided more opportunity to act it out.

The provocative equipment provided by the teachers fulfilled the children's need to lift things, scaffolded their learning about how ropes and pulleys and weight work together, and demanded a response. When someone is stuck in old ways of trying things, new materials can be a powerful prod to try something new. In this case, children quickly learned how much weight ropes can lift when combined with a pulley and how efficient hooks can be, while teachers learned that experienced facilitators can lend expertise and new experiences that facilitate new ways of doing things.

Provisioning the Environment

How does your physical environment support children's learning about their topic of interest through play? Educators in Reggio Emilia refer to the environment as the third teacher (the parent being the first and the teacher being the second). In *Designs for Living and Learning,* Deb Curtis ande Margie Carter point out, "Children often come up with thoughts about how they want to use materials or space, and in many cases this is different than what the teachers originally envisioned" (2003, 55). It is clear that when we provision the environment with inviting materials (for example, found objects, loose parts, and reference materials) in response to children's ideas, we can be taken by surprise. It's at this point that we need to step back to observe further, let go, and see what happens. Children are often more creative than we are, and we can learn from them if we remain open-minded.

You may choose to enrich one particular area of your classroom if it connects to an idea the children have. Or, if a large group of children is taking their topic into many classroom areas, you may need to change the whole room. Let's look at a couple of examples.

Building in the Art Area

In a preschool program, one child has begun, on a small scale, to build with recyclables in the art area. He talks with a teacher about an idea he has for creating a playground, and later in the day she ensures that a greater variety of building materials (cardboard, clay, pipe cleaners, spools, empty film canisters, materials from nature, and so on) is accessible in this area. Also, so the structure can be moved and saved as needed over a long period of time, she provides a very large piece of cardboard to build on. Over a period of several days, the child constructs a complete playground with swings, slides, and climbing structures. Other children come and go as he works, and although they don't want to build a playground themselves, they do watch carefully, ask questions, and gather ideas about how to use loose parts that later appear in their own constructions.

Drama Everywhere

A large group of children spends all of their playtime, every day, engaged in dramatic play in all areas of the classroom. Their play is varied and follows no particular topic, so the teaching team has to think hard about how to support it. They decide to offer more opportunities for creativity by providing a dramatic play area that is more open ended. That is, the physical setup is not supposed to be a house or a vet's office or a hospital. They remove furniture and props that have obvious purposes (stove, bed, and so on) and replace them with large cardboard boxes, lengths of fabric, Bear Blocks (large wooden blocks covered with carpet), sheets, and many small loose parts such as spools, pillows, and short branches. Now, with many more possibilities opened up, children can more effectively play out absolutely any idea that comes to mind. This change lasts for several weeks, until the children's play focus veers in another direction. Interestingly, at no time during this change do the children ask where the other play furniture has gone.

In each of these examples, rather than thinking about what is supposed to happen in traditional areas of the room, the teachers instead responded to what was actually happening. The ideas of one child often can be missed within the many types of group projects that are under way. And in the opposite vein, group ideas for play sometimes can be left to take their own course, without support.

When considering a change in the environment in response to observation and reflection, you might ask yourself whether the children need more props in order to play out their ideas, or more space, or more materials to represent their thinking. If the answer is yes, then working with the environment becomes a good option.

When a teacher provisions the environment in response to the children, their classrooms cease to follow the script of how to set up an early childhood classroom. Instead, it becomes an environment for this particular group of children, or this one child, thus supporting both learning and interest. Such a classroom is rich with possibility.

Taking the Children Out of the Classroom

In observing children's play, you may notice misunderstandings that could be clarified by a trip to a workplace, or by watching someone with a particular set of skills in action. Or maybe the children are seeking information the teachers do not have at their fingertips, but could be provided elsewhere. When answers or a deepening of knowledge can be found elsewhere, it is time to leave the classroom and explore the broader world. This may involve making a visit to another classroom or group of children, or it might be something more adventurous involving a field trip. Here are two examples of teachers taking children out of the classroom to explore an idea.

Babies

Children in the preschool room at CFDC were fascinated with babies. When the little ones came to visit their siblings in the preschool room, the older children would immediately change their way of speaking to parentese, that natural singsong manner of speaking that is so engaging for infants. Intrigued by this, the preschool teachers gave the children the opportunity to discuss ideas about how babies learned to speak, asking questions such as "How did you learn to talk?" and "Do babies copy us when we speak?" and to regularly visit the infant room to interact with the infants—a precursor to a later, in-depth study of communication.

Camping at School

When a child at University Children's Center in Halifax spontaneously brought in a sleeping bag, a whole summer's worth of play and learning began. Cathy Ramos, program coordinator at that time, tells what happened:

> The children now wanted to go camping. We began a brainstorming session with them, discussing what they already knew and what they wanted to learn. Later, the teachers discussed how they could engage with the children and expand on this interest. Soon, there was a campground in the corner of the room. There was a tent with sleeping bags, outdoor carpet for grass, and a campfire the children made out of tissue ("red and yellow and orange because you need all those colors for a fire") and pieces of wood. We purchased camp hats and lanterns at a dollar store and some inexpensive camping dishes from a department store. Since we didn't have a checkered tablecloth and the children insisted we needed one, they made one by drawing squares on plain white paper and filling them in. The biggest challenge was how to go camping at night, for that was what the children wanted. The teachers helped them hang up black garbage bags and the children spent days cutting out stars to stick on the bags. After instructing the teachers on how to make the Big Dipper, they had a stargazing party. We hung up a blue tarp ("in case it rains"). This play went on for the whole summer, and they never tired of it. Instead the

children and teachers continued to think together about new things they needed to learn to go camping. Continuing discussion about what you need to eat on a camping trip resulted in a big barbecue.

When the children's talk changed to rock climbing, we teachers felt this was a challenge. We asked ourselves, "How do we safely support this?" We made some calls and were delighted when Mountain Equipment Co-op in Halifax agreed to let us come and use their rock wall. The children were so excited and talked for days about what they needed to wear and what equipment they needed to go rock climbing. It was quite an adventure—even the shyest child surprised us by climbing higher than we thought he would. The staff at the store were amazing. They spent the whole morning with us, supporting the climb, ensuring that we were safe, showing us how to put up a tent, and demonstrating other camping materials.

We made a video and revisited that trip over and over again. What a summer! We were sad when it drew to a close and interests pointed in other directions. Of course, one of those directions was "mountain climbing on real mountains." We'll need some time to think of a way we can support that!

A whole new world of experiences opens up when we take children outside our program. Teachers must carefully consider destinations in terms of hands-on learning experiences, and certainly should visit the facility first in order to get the most out of a field trip. Ask yourself: How can the hosts become involved in sharing their expertise? How comfortable will they be with this role? What can the children actually do there? If field trips are beyond your reach, take a look at your own facility and the immediate surrounding area. What opportunities exist for visiting another room and using the expertise of older children? The cook? The groundskeeper? Those who do repairs on the facility?

What Are They Learning?

- **Self-esteem**. The children at this center have received an important message: their ideas will be taken up by teachers and supported.

- **Resourcefulness**. When materials do not exist in the classroom, they can be made.

- **Science**. The children both shared their prior knowledge about constellations and further developed that knowledge.

- **Social competence**. The children were able to enter the local community in a meaningful way and take on the challenge of climbing in a safe environment.

- **Problem solving and negotiation**. Plans for big events can be negotiated, shared, and carried out.

Inviting an Expert to Visit

When the children's interest lies outside your own expertise, it makes sense not only to research the topic but also to invite in other professionals to spend time with the children, share their skills, and answer the children's questions. Doing so makes a topic real to children and introduces them to new possibilities. Consider the following examples.

Since the children are experimenting with making designs for their buildings, the teachers invite a child's mom who is an architect to the classroom. She spends a couple of hours building with children in the block area and shows them some of her blueprints. The children then go on to examine the blueprints of their own school.

When the children are interested in animals, a parent who works at a local zoo brings in a snake and a parakeet to support the children's investigations. On another occasion, the children visit a parent who is a dog groomer and watch her as she bathes and clips a dog. As a result, dog grooming becomes a part of their play repertoire in the classroom.

Some of the children have shown an interest in painting with a variety of tools. A local amateur artist comes in to paint alongside the children. He shares techniques and encourages the children to pursue their own directions in art using new tools and approaches.

After a nature walk, a dad who is a member of a local nature preservation group brings in samples of moss, plants, abandoned nests, and so on. He spends the play period casually talking with children about these artifacts. The children use a feely bag to try to identify the items.

Such visitors may scaffold children's learning in ways that early childhood educators cannot. Teachers, after all, generally are not architects or zoo keepers. Teachers can, however, bring the children and these professionals together, resulting in an expansion of not only the children's learning but also their own.

Organizing Children

As we observe, it becomes clear to us whether one child, a handful of children, or the whole group is taking the play in a particular direction. Several clues can help lead teachers to a conclusion about how many children are interested in which play ideas. They all depend on good observation over a period of at least several days—you need to see how the play scenarios play out. As an example, consider a child in the block area at Jubilee Road Children's Center. He took half an hour, on two consecutive days, to carefully and precisely fit all the small cars into a small wooden wagon.

Although other children had glanced with interest as they worked around him and teachers found the work fascinating, no other children picked up on this idea, even after the staff set out other invitations. After agreeing that this was interesting only to this one child, we decided to document his work so that he could talk about it further and could try other ways of fitting small objects into larger spaces.

You may, on the other hand, find four or five children who are deeply engaged in play around a topic. If, for instance, several children check every single day to see how their seeds are progressing, and seek out charts and books about growth as a reference, this would be an opportunity to work with this small group at a particular time of day. By photographing their seeds on a regular basis, revisiting these photographs with the children, and offering many ways to measure and record the growth of their plants, children will have a lasting and satisfying record. Indirectly, they will also be developing some math skills.

In my experience, the younger the children are, the less likely it is that they will be engaged in whole-group projects, even though from time to time a topic that captures everyone's interest and imagination may arise. For instance, a whole group of three- to five-year-olds at one center became engaged with measuring. What began with a few children measuring their buildings grew to an exploration of all the tools that could be used for measuring, as well as all of the things that could be measured. This large topic appealed to all ages and developmental levels, in part because all children could identify with the idea of growth and size.

There are ways to adapt the daily routine and activities to differing interests: consider supporting individual children in their own ideas; create small group times for small groups of children to work together on an idea of mutual interest; and bring the whole group together to share ideas through large-group meetings.

Supporting Individual Children

You can support a single child playing by herself by providing appropriate materials, touching base with her from time to time to offer support, engaging her in conversation about what she is doing, and referring other children to her as the opportunity arises. As she works, it's important to document what she is doing, just as one would for groups of children, and to revisit her work with her so she can tell you more about her thinking. The documentation also can be used to share her work with other children at large-group times. The children might be invited to ask questions or offer ideas.

When children are working hard on an individual project, they often worry about their work being safe from other children. Here you can play a protective role, offering to place the work on a safe shelf from day to day or, if the work has to be taken down for some reason, you can make a quick sketch or take a photograph of the work for the child. In planning for individual work, it is important to think about where the work will take place. A small table is often useful, but some individual work can happen at a large table with other children engaged in their own activities, if the children are comfortable with this.

Small Groups

Small groups are ideal for project work and provide an opportunity for learning that is child initiated while framed by the teacher. Some centers have a daily routine that includes more formal small-group times during which all children divide into groups to work on projects at a certain time of day. Other centers choose to make this time informal, with small-group work occurring during play. Still others might take a small group of children to an area for specific project work while other children who are not involved in the project continue with their play. How the small-group work occurs probably isn't as important as having the flexibility for children to work on special topics when they come up, in a group size that is conducive to thinking and talking together, with support from a teacher.

Being in large groups throughout the entire day is quite stressful for children. To sometimes be in small groups—either during formal small-group times as part of the daily routine, or more informally around the room during playtimes—provides a break from the hustle and bustle of the larger group. It provides an opportunity for either teacher-led activities that tie into children's interests or for child-initiated projects.

In some classrooms, such as the preschool room at Peter Green Hall Children's Center, children are given the choice of which small group they wish to join on any given day. The children are introduced to the options at a large-group gathering and then choose the activities that interest them.

Other settings that have regular small-group times have children stay in the same small groups for the long term, according to development or interests, so they have the continuity of being with the same children and the same teacher each day. So, while one group might be working on constructing an environment for the class hamster, another might be researching how to build a tree house, and a third group might be exploring the attributes of watercolor. As children finish their small-group work, teachers often make the materials available within the classroom so all children have access to them.

All of these options are valid, and the teachers' decisions about how they will provide for small-group work will depend on the children's ideas and questions, the space available, and the nature of the daily routine.

Whole Groups

When all the children are excited about or interested in a broad topic, teachers may decide that it's worth a whole-group investigation. Getting to know the community, for instance, would lend itself to class field trips. Within that exploration, there may be small groups of children who want to follow up on specific topics such as mail, garbage collection, the bakery, or the fire station. Often there are play topics that recur or last over several weeks, signaling that some deeper investigation is called for, or that some extensions to the play might be offered.

Whole-group interests might be explored in various ways, several of which we have already addressed: provisioning the environment, inviting a visitor to share expertise, taking a field trip (which can also be done in small groups), or perhaps doing research using classroom resources. In addition, we need to remember the "hundred languages of children" (Edwards, Gandini, and Forman 1993) and offer them many ways to share what they know. Large-group meetings might address an interest or exploration through revisiting documentation, music, drama, language charts, or webbing. Project work or many opportunities to use graphic materials can show children's understanding. And story times provide the chance for discovery for the whole group through literature, with opportunities for teachers to note children's questions and comments.

By listening to children's comments during large-group times, you can sometimes discover topics for small-group work. In this way, whole-group work can support small-group work, and small-group work can extend and deepen a large-group topic.

With any of these approaches it's always vital to continue observing and reflecting on what is happening—not what you planned to happen, but what actually did happen! These are often two quite different scenarios, and we must strive to keep an open mind. Here is an example of a plan that changed and how a different small-group time emerged.

At circle time in preschool, Lori provides an opportunity for exploring "beginning, middle, and end." She had noticed an interest in storytelling among the children and wondered what they know about stories.

> As I enter the preschool room, I see children standing on a masking tape line within their circle. They're talking about where the line starts and ends, and who's in the middle. Once the children are seated again, Lori shows them three illustrations from a familiar sequential storybook. "Which picture do you think comes first," she asks, "and which one comes next?" Seeing the children struggle with this, Lori rereads the familiar tale, which helps the children decide on the sequence of the illustrations.
>
> Soon, another teacher is showing me some paper puppets that three children made that morning at the writing table. They are incredibly detailed, even partially 3-D in their construction. I note that these children are in my small group, which is coming up next. What if I could connect what Lori was doing in circle time with what these children did in making paper puppets? I think of Vivian Paley, who describes back to children what she's seen them do during play. What if, I wonder, the children told their story of building puppets with a beginning, a middle, and an end?
>
> I put my original small-group plans on hold, while chart paper and drawing paper are gathered. At small-group time, the children are invited to tell how they made "these wonderful puppets." They do this with enthusiasm, and I write down their words and read them back. Then, they draw their puppets. One of the children draws a puppet theater instead, and I'm led to think about the possibilities that may stem from this.

Do you recognize the flexibility involved in this decision? In order to bring together an interest in building puppets and the idea of sequencing, I had to change my original plan right there. Though such on-the-spot decisions and changes aren't required for emergent curriculum, flexibility of thinking is a disposition that helps teachers take creative steps toward truly child-centered curriculum.

Writing Down the Plan

In my conversations with teachers who use emergent curriculum, a puzzle is always present: How do we write down the plan in advance (which is often required by licensing authorities) when we aren't yet sure exactly what is emerging? By 2006, the staff at the

CFDC had been wrestling with this challenge for some time. They had explored several designs, played with formats, and field-tested the options. They always tried to represent the dynamic nature of emergent curriculum by showing the observations in each area, the thinking that the teachers did, and their responses in the form of next steps. Here is one of the ways they recorded what they expected would happen over the next few days. Keep in mind that they were trying to document not only the plan but also the how and why of the plan; that is, the rationale behind it. Two planning formats are represented below, one for the infant room, and one for the preschool room.

Infant Room Planning

In the infant room, the one-year-olds often imitate adult roles in their play. After setting up the water table with dolls and sponges for baby washing, one day Carrie observed that the children were not as interested in washing the dolls as they were in washing tabletops and furniture. This made sense, for the older infants had seen Carrie complete this adult work. Using a newly developed planning format, Carrie documented her observations and the children's responses.

Infant Room, January 31 Previous observation and plan in response	Follow-up notes after watching children's responses to materials
Rationale: Yesterday, many of the children were interested in washing the table and the floor, rather than the babies.	**Observation:** Today the children enjoyed squeezing sponges and watching them drip. Greta took a sponge to the table to wipe with, and Peter and Peyton followed and did the same.
Activity in response: cleaning based on role play; introduce sponges **Sensory:** washcloths with dishes, cleaning and washing with water and suds **Motor skills:** fine-motor—squeezing; gross-motor—large wiping movements **Social learning:** watching others for ideas of what to do with the materials	

On the following day, teachers continued to follow up on the use of sponges:

Infant Room, February 1 Previous observations and plan in response	Follow-up notes after watching children's responses to materials
Rationale: Yesterday, instead of washing dishes, the sponges themselves were of more interest. The children carried them around, washing tabletops and other furniture.	**Observation:** Today the children used the sponges at both water stations. They took the sponges, walked around the classroom with them, and wrung them out on the tile floor. They wiped furniture and each other.
Activity added in response: we added an extra cabinet with a small bucket for water **Sensory:** water in the sensory table, plus water in the bucket, both with sponges **Motor skills:** gross-motor—washing with large arm movements; fine-motor—squeezing sponges **Social learning:** following the adult model, watching and following each other, sometimes taking turns with sponges	

Preschool Planning

Meanwhile, in the preschool room—after dozens of attempts—the teachers came up with the following format, with a separate planning sheet for each area of the classroom. A different teacher is responsible for each of these areas, on a rotating basis. Within each area, the teacher observes, interacts with children, provisions and maintains the environment, and then takes the observations to the team for discussion. Here's a sample plan for just one area of the room—the art area:

Art area: Katie
Monday
Observation: A child in the art area uses paper cups to build a structure
Teacher's thinking: We have lots of donated paper cups. Can we use them for large-scale construction? Would the children take up this invitation? How would their building change?
Activity/scaffolding for tomorrow: Set up invitation in the block area and observe use of cups

And here is what happened in the block area on Tuesday, after the teachers issued their invitation to use the cups for building.

These two sample formats illustrate how difficult it can be to devise a way of writing down curriculum as it evolves. These formats are an experiment showing the teachers' thinking about what they've seen and what they will do. Other schools use other formats. Many choose not to use fill-in-the-box forms, because they tend to limit one's thinking. Instead, teachers might try curriculum webs,

flowcharts, time lines, or even daily pages in a log book to show what happened and why. This latter idea demonstrates Betty Jones's position that "curriculum is best written down after the fact" (B. Jones, pers. comm.). For many teachers, though, the reality is that they have to write curriculum plans in advance. Finding the right format is a work in progress, and we must aim for flexibility and innovation.

The Teacher's Voice: Puppy Play

When teachers are considering the perspectives of each teacher as well as those of the individual children, it is inevitable that there will be different opinions and ideas. This can be a positive situation, since it opens teachers' minds to ideas and interpretations they might never have thought of. All ideas can be considered, discussed, and perhaps even used. Usually there is not one right response to what is going on in the classroom, but several.

Let's revisit the puppy play mentioned in the last chapter. You may recall that the staff found this play idea puzzling and somewhat irritating. They weren't sure how to respond to it. When we left the team, Lori had gathered input from the Emergent Curriculum Collaborative. Before we catch up with the team, however, Lori will explain the format of this team's meetings, and how decisions are usually made.

We meet several times a week during naptime to reflect. Our sessions are a cross between a meeting of the minds and a Ping-Pong match! The team has a common

focus. In this case, our question was, "Why animals?" We treat such a question as the beginning of teacher research.

Because the teachers work in zones within the classroom, each has a different perspective and set of observations to bring to the meeting for consideration. We're always observing different facets of children's play: story lines, development, misconceptions, questions, problem solving, how the environment is working for the children, and so on, all while being mindful of the common topic.

When reflecting, we start by zone, and after a teacher shares observations we might ask something such as "What does this make you think about?" Here's where the Ping-Pong match comes into play. Just when you think you know which way the path is leading, a new perspective adds to the complexity and makes you rethink your original idea or understanding!

One might think that after meeting with the collaborative, things became clearer for Lori and her team. Instead, at first, there was some disequilibrium.

When I presented the data to the team, their moans of disapproval and negativity ("the kids are going to be wild") revealed their ambivalence about delving into the topic. My enthusiasm, however, was contagious! I shared with them the list of thoughts from the group, and suggested we use them to guide our research, employing observation and invitations to find out more. They agreed to start small, using only the sensory table for an animal scenario (a controlled invitation). This was definitely a compromise; and ocean animals and props were added to the water in the sensory table.

Now, rather than treating puppy play as a problem or difficulty, there is a way in, via a small invitation in the sensory table, that is a compromise for some of the teachers. What is important here is that their lead teacher (their provocateur) suggests that they engage in research about this play. The idea of watching the play in the sensory table through the eyes of a researcher offers these teachers a new approach to observing the play and digging deeper as they try to understand what these children find so fascinating.

At the next meeting, the team members once more brought along their observations from the different areas of the classroom. Since the last meeting, more varieties of animals had been offered to the children, and some children had started using the materials in the sensory table. Here we see the team's efforts to think of all the possible responses to observations from three different areas.

Bonnie (dramatic play zone)

Observation: When children are given toy animals (including dogs) to play with, they cease to become animals.

Teachers' thinking: Do toys become a catalyst for children's ideas? Is it easier to pretend with a toy than to act the idea out, or vice versa? Are the children's story lines the same or different? Do they use the toy animals in ways that are consistent with the toys?

Response: We decided to observe this more. And, to see what the response or change would be, we decided to experiment with limiting or even removing toy animals and puppy paraphernalia. Also, to gauge the level of interest, we decided to create an invitation for animal-specific habitats.

Lori (block zone)

Observation: The children have started building "zoo trains," and ever since that began, no tall buildings have been built.

Teachers' thinking: Where is the zoo and do the animals ever arrive? Following some discussion, we realized that the children have been grouping the animals on the train by species. Sorting, graphing, and charting come to mind. The groupings also include enclosures for the animals. Are these cages? Or habitats?

Response: We decided to offer invitations for exploring both the relationships between different animals and their habitats and the children's ability to categorize. We also decided to add pond animals to the African animals in the block area to observe how the children would react to these two very different habitats.

Katie (studio arts zone)

Observation: The children are repeatedly lining up chairs for an audience to watch a dog show.

Teachers' thinking: This type of play demonstrates the children's prior experiences with shows. We know that some children have taken dance lessons or have attended a play. We wonder if we might build on this by helping the children to build a stage. Since we do not have a lot of space, there is concern that the stage will be overstimulating for this area due to crowding the space. What about puppet play?

Response: We decide to offer an invitation to create puppets for acting out stories, including materials that could be used to create puppy puppets.

We see that the team of teachers went through several phases of reflection during this time. They observed constantly, writing about the children in several different play areas of the room. They then tried to analyze and interpret what was going on (What is this about? Why puppies?). In an effort to reach deeper understanding, they included others in this discussion. They also thought about the implications of their own feelings about this lively play. They found it perplexing and sometimes irritating. Rather than simply putting a stop to the play, however, they tried to find a reason for their own feelings and a compromise that would work for both teachers and the children. Finally, through invitations and further discussion, they found a way into the play that widened the children's ideas, respected the children who still wanted to play puppies, and felt manageable to them. Although it was not a perfect solution in terms of fully accepting the children's play or completely understanding it, the teachers thought hard about this play. They also learned something about their own boundaries for lively and noisy play.

The Child's Voice: The Traveling Classroom

Next consider a situation that absolutely baffled the same group of teachers over a period of weeks. Although they never did discover the root of the children's idea, their teaching practice was made richer from the experience of letting go.

Twenty-one preschool children in a richly provisioned environment suddenly began collecting materials from around the room—markers, dolls, small blocks, natural materials, whatever—and moving them to other places in the room. To the teachers' dismay, and for days on end, huge piles of mixed-up classroom materials formed in the center of the room, or in the block area.

Teachers generally are organized people. For this team, the children's purposeful disorganization of the classroom interfered with their desire to keep an organized and attractive room. Compounding the struggle was the children's natural reluctance to clean up afterward. This was a task of mammoth proportions.

The teachers decided to engage the children in conversations about their play and intentions. Had any of the children recently moved to a different house? It seemed not. Were they perhaps exploring classification? No. They tended to pile everything up together in a big heap. Was this about power over their own environment? Perhaps. Discussing this idea further, the teachers settled on asking the children how they would like to arrange the classroom. Although this resulted in a major furniture and materials shift according to the children's ideas, the moving and piling up of materials continued.

After weeks of documentation, thinking together, and many cleanup times that lasted forty-five minutes, the teachers realized they might never get to the bottom of this play idea. What they knew for certain was that the children were focused on moving stuff and that this in itself provided enough intrinsic motivation to keep them engaged for almost six weeks. Although this focus, which the teachers called "the traveling classroom," wore them out, they also learned something about the children's learning, as well as their own, during the process.

- Children cannot always articulate their ideas. Staff have to document through photography, notes, and artifacts, and then use their best educated guess in order to respond.

- Teachers do not always have to know why in order to support play. In this case, teachers offered large baskets with handles in order to make carrying easier, and pulleys so children could move things around the room. They also continuously engaged with children as they worked.

- Children learned to work hard together. There was much fetching and carrying, as well as heavy lifting that required more than one child, and therefore lots of negotiation.

- Children made plans and carried them out. They demonstrated intentionality.

- Problem solving the cleanup times was a large part of this play. The children and teachers met at circle time to brainstorm together ways to handle the big cleanup jobs and make them less tedious.

- An incredible amount of classifying took place as children cleaned up—not only through organizing materials to be returned to their containers and shelves, but also in other ways: "Nora will pick up all the writing area stuff" or "James will find all the little toy people."

- Teachers learned that even though they were uncomfortable with what children were doing, they could nonetheless maintain their sense of humor as well as flexibility and responsiveness while still recognizing the learning that was taking place. Even though not completely understandable to teachers, the play was engaging and purposeful for the children.

As we have seen, interpretation of our observations can be challenging for teachers. It's also stimulating to think about our ideas together. During puzzling times at our school, it was not unusual for me, as the director, to witness the team engaged in very lively discussion as they talked about what was happening and how to respond. There was often laughter, exclamations, and thoughtful expressions as teachers pondered the options, and then shouts of excitement as they recognized one of those lovely "aha" moments when new understanding breaks through. Such deep consideration of children's ideas for play produces stimulation, intellectual engagement, and passion. We couldn't ask for more in our work with children and each other.

Suggested Readings

Chard, S. 1998. *The Project Approach: Making Curriculum Come Alive.* New York: Scholastic.

Katz, L., and S. Chard. 2000. *Engaging Children's Minds: The Project Approach.* Greenwich, Conn.: Ablex.

Stacey, S. 2001. Coaching Community Hosts: The Other Side of the Field Trip. *Child Care Information Exchange* 5:48–51.

6

Documentation— Making Thinking Visible

As I leaf through a classroom folder, I find an assortment of intriguing artifacts: sticky notes with brief anecdotes scribbled by three teachers, a transcript of a conversation between three children as they play at being puppies, a teacher's description of a "dog show" put on by children, a hastily written list of questions about the children's play from a teacher on this team (with a reminder to herself to "think outside the box!"), "notes to self" about how children are playing, a transcript of children in conversation about building an animal hospital, a curriculum web of brainstormed ideas about possibilities for future directions, notes with provocations written by teachers to themselves ("provide more challenges—how?!"), samples of children's work (puppets they've made, drawings, photos of clay work and other models, writing samples), columns of brainstorming that has been done with children about animals of various types, and, finally, photographs— lots and lots of photographs of children at play, the investigations they've been working on, and the structures and artifacts they've created, including photos of the process by which they were made.

Such a diverse and wonderful collection of materials is not just bits and pieces. Rather, it's a gold mine of precious information about the work and thinking of teachers and children as they collaborated in the classroom. In this particular instance, it's the raw material for constructing the story of what happened during the puppy/animal play that engaged the children so completely over a period of weeks. These traces of everyone's work are perfect for communicating to others what the classroom work was all about, how it unfolded, what the teachers' thinking was in response, what the children and teachers learned, and how they constructed this knowledge. In other words, these materials are the essential and exciting data for assembling documentation.

Why is documentation such a useful tool when generating emergent curriculum? As we will see in this chapter, documentation is a visual or written record or both that shows traces of the children's work, our thinking as teachers, the activities and learning that have been taking place in the classroom, and, most important, the process that children and teachers have gone through to construct knowledge or develop new understandings.

Documentation is important because it tells the story of a project, an ordinary moment, the development of an idea, intriguing or puzzling events, or anything else that a teacher feels is essential to communicate to others or to hold onto so that it becomes part of the history of the classroom or school.

In addition, early childhood educators are frequently required to provide records of what they've covered in their curriculum. If this is a requirement within your organization, then documentation provides a child-centered route to accountability; children's work is documented, explained, and made accessible. Their interests, as well as the learning that has taken place through exploration and investigation of those interests, are made explicit in an engaging and meaningful format.

In this chapter we explore the many reasons to document. We also look at the practicalities of putting it all together using simple systems within your classroom, so you can communicate both the children's thinking about what is happening and your own.

Why Document?

Documentation requires time, thought, and energy. When I consult with early childhood professionals, their first query to me often is, "Why would I want to do this?" My response is to ask teachers to create just a small piece of documentation, think about it with others, and see how that feels. As I watch the process unfold, I almost always see excitement, interesting discussions, and meaningful dialogue between teachers. I also see a very useful piece of work being shared with others, validating the work of both teachers and children. Below, we explore documentation's role in reflection, accountability, communication, and validation.

A Tool for Reflection

Within the process of generating emergent curriculum, documentation is a tool that engages teachers in reflective practice. As we consider the artifacts, photos, and notes we have collected, we are pushed to make some meaning out of what is happening or what has already happened in the classroom. What is important about this event or project, and why? What do we want to preserve or communicate, and why? How should this documentation be presented and shared? As a team sifts through the materials and reflects on these questions, a kind of magnifying glass seems to appear to help us examine the details. How an idea unfolded, the process of discovery, and the puzzles and struggles as children construct knowledge all become visible. Artifacts and notes can lead us to this type of thinking because they provide us with something concrete to react to and think about. Examining the concrete often enables us to move to the abstract: What is this really all about? What is under the surface? Are there any patterns or connections emerging? What can we learn from this small moment or that larger event?

The process of teachers learning from documentation is another important piece of this system. As professionals who seek continuous growth, we need intellectual stimulation. Documentation is a tool for encouraging interpretation and for making connections, hypotheses, and plans for future work. Documentation often makes our own learning visible to us, and this can be very rewarding. What we didn't understand six months ago may suddenly become clear in another situation at another time as we look back on our documentation and rethink it. This can be a transformative experience for teachers, in that we are no longer depending solely on outside sources for our growth, but instead are using our documentation—and our thinking about it—to inform our own teaching.

For the student teacher, documentation can be an important tool for learning about child development, teaching methods, and curriculum development. Quality documentation requires thinking about where the child is developmentally, what the child is trying to do, and how teachers support this quest, and then forming connections between theory and practice. All of this provides an excellent foundation for future teaching.

Accountability

Regardless of the kind of setting teachers work in, they are accountable to others for showing what children are doing, how they are developing, what interests them, who their friends are, and what they are learning. While some early childhood settings have a specific assessment tool they must use, others are free to develop their own approaches.

At first glance, completing an assessment of children's development in a play-based classroom that uses emergent approaches may seem challenging. But through its many forms, documentation provides an extremely detailed collection that shows parents and administration what each child is doing and how this work aids in the child's growth, development, and learning. It also demonstrates how each child negotiates and works with others, follows through on an idea, makes connections between experiences, and makes his or her thinking visible through representation with varied media. This important information is likely to be more meaningful for a parent than a checklist, which may include unfamiliar jargon, and is less intimidating than a rating scale. And documentation generally is nonjudgmental, since it describes what the child can do, rather than what she cannot yet accomplish.

Communication

As a tool for communication, documentation has no equal. It's useful for helping parents understand their own child's work within the context of the larger group. It helps children look back and reflect on their thinking, questions, and theories. It is a remarkable way of communicating the capabilities of young children and the value of teachers' work to the wider community.

For parents, entering a school and seeing photographs of children at work, together with background information, is extremely enticing. Although naturally enchanted by their own child's work, they also become drawn into the work of the whole school as they begin to understand the thinking that is taking place behind the scenes. Also, they may see that their own child is affected by everything that takes place within the classroom, including the work and learning of other children (Fraser and Gestwicki 2002).

Understanding the process of how children are learning within your classroom makes it easier for parents to become involved in the life of the school. When parents show interest in a piece of documentation, they can be invited to offer ideas of their own, jot down their questions, share their knowledge or expertise, or contribute to the documentation process with photography, artifacts, or recordings. Parents who cannot spend time at school due to work or other commitments may be able to make recordings of stories that relate to the children's work, take photographs around the city that will support an investigation, or write brief notes to you about what their child has said at home about the work at school. Such contributions can help us create collaborations and deepen the relationships between teacher, parent, and child.

Because children love to examine and explain their own work, revisiting their work through documentation—whether in panel, video, or book form—is an easy way to facilitate discussions with preschool children. Toddlers are also delighted to label what they see happening in photographs. And infants will sometimes point to the real artifact in the room when presented with a photograph of the artifact. Seeing that documentation provokes connections for children of all ages is exciting for teachers, since we can build upon those connections.

It is obvious that we should be sharing our work with the community. Unfortunately, even though early childhood education and early brain development generate interest and attention on many fronts, both remain poorly understood by those outside our field. Documentation can be a valuable communication tool in addressing this issue. When we show the deep meaning of what we do, how it benefits young children, and the expertise of those who care for and educate our youngest citizens, everyone benefits.

Validation

In a profession where respect for our work is sometimes sadly lacking, documentation makes clear the careful thinking, painstaking attention to detail, continuous observation, and engagement with children that take place every day. It validates the work of both the children and the teachers. It is a process that helps generate respect for what we do. Although campaigns, political action, and advocacy have been under way for years, we sometimes need to remind ourselves of the importance of what we do. If you have never attempted documentation, you are in for a pleasant surprise. Seeing your work with children presented in a graphic format is a validating experience; it can help you remain passionate about your work.

Collecting Data for Documentation

There are many types of documentation, and what you choose to do within your own classroom will depend largely on resources such as time, funding, and support. When we speak of the data for documentation, we are talking about such items as photographs, children's work samples, anecdotal notes, and audio/video recordings.

Photography

Digital photography has changed the process of documenting children's work, in that digital photographs are instant, can easily be edited, and can be printed on-site. This efficient process means that we keep only the photos that are truly meaningful for telling the story. It also allows us to produce documentation without much delay, so children and parents can see and think about the work in a timely fashion. (For points to remember about using photography for documentation, see chapter 2.)

With adult support, children can photograph what they consider important. They might choose to photograph other children, the projects they have been working on, areas of the classroom, and, of course, their teachers. When the decision is the children's, the results can be interesting for teachers. Sometimes what we consider to be an important part of the child's day is not what the child chooses to document, and this offers much food for thought.

Video and Audio Recordings

In a staff or team meeting, it's always interesting to notice how much more becomes clear to us when we watch a short piece of videotape or listen to a recorded conversation. We may think we notice everything that goes on around us, but inevitably there are surprises and enlightenment when teachers use recordings of play as a form of documentation. Sections of audiotape can be transcribed to make visible the dialogue between children that explains their idea or learning, and pieces of videotape (especially when played on a laptop near the room entrance) will provide talking points for all who watch. These types of documentation are also useful as a supplement to a child's portfolio, or when showing is better than telling (when, for instance, an event is difficult to describe in words), or when teachers need documentation for reflection purposes.

Collections of Children's Work

Teachers are great collectors of children's work—but so are the children, who often want to take home what they've created. Photocopying children's art or writing samples is one option, and photographing their sculptures and buildings is another. If none of these options is available, teachers can always make a quick sketch.

There are some important decisions to be made in terms of which pieces of children's work to use for documentation. When you have several artifacts to choose from (for example, drawings, photos of clay work or paintings, transcriptions of dialogue), ask yourself the following questions:

- Which pieces actually move the story of the process forward?

- Which pieces represent something unusual, perplexing, or new in the exploration?

- Which pieces raise interesting questions for teachers or for other children?

- Can you find traces of dialogue from children that would help to explain their thinking?

- Are photographs needed, or can the work samples tell the story? If photos are needed, how many actually make visible a part of the process?

- Are there any teachers' notes that would help viewers make meaning out of what they are seeing?

Forms of Documentation

Documentation—the assembling and presentation of artifacts, dialogue transcripts, and records of teachers' and children's thinking—can take many forms. And different forms of documentation are suitable for different circumstances and settings. Here is an overview of some of the formats you can choose from.

Daily Pages

A daily page consists of an interesting photograph (or perhaps two) coupled with a typed paragraph by a teacher that explains the team's thinking about what is happening. Rather than trying to capture all the children, the photo focuses on one child or a small group of children at work. Neither teachers nor parents worry too much about which child is featured, for over time, all of the children are represented. The teacher who is working on the page always tries to point out the

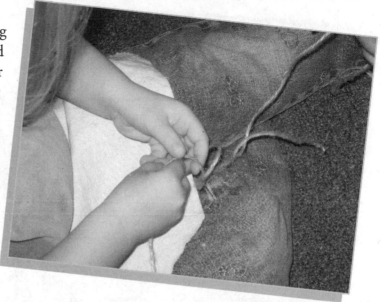

learning that is taking place. After much practice, the family room staff at CFDC are now able to print out a photograph and type a paragraph in about twenty minutes. They find that parents consistently read their daily page. In fact, parents so look forward to this snippet of classroom life that many are in the habit of stopping to read it when they pick up their child at the end of the day.

School Log

Building further upon the idea of a daily page, Emerson Preschool has developed the school log into fine art. They place their beautiful and detailed record of children's work and daily events at the entrance to the school as an invitation to parents to read about the children's morning when they pick up their children at midday. Responsibility for the log rotates among teachers. The teacher who is classroom documenter for the week carries the camera around and writes anecdotes while moving among the children. At the end of the morning this teacher chooses what to use and assembles the page. The finished page is then placed in the log book (a large three-ring binder).

The log book is also the school's archive. It illustrates the vitality and life of the school, the care with which children's work is treated, and the seriousness with which that work is displayed. The school's director, Susan Hagner, says, "I usually take the log book with me to our meetings. It helps us to remember and reflect" (S. Hagner, pers. comm.). She also explains that each teacher constructs the log in a different way, using his or her own strengths and talents, so each teacher's personality is visible in different areas of the log.

Curriculum Paths

For long-term projects, a curriculum path can show us where we've been so far, and where we may be headed. Looking something like a flowchart, a curriculum path probably is best created in an as-we-go manner on a long, horizontal sheet of paper so that the full scope of the project can be represented in large print. For the Garden Project at CFDC, for instance, the beginning point was the development of the outdoor classroom. The children's ideas were written in one color, input from the community in another, and teacher planning for activities and events in a third. Since this project lasted for about three months, the curriculum path eventually extended to a length of about eight feet and showed every aspect of the journey in written form.

Documentation Panels

When children and teachers have been working on a long-term investigation, several sequential documentation panels can tell the whole story. A documentation panel, first introduced to us by the teachers of Reggio Emilia, is a thoughtful collection of writing, photos, and artifacts mounted on a panel made of foam board, posterboard, Plexiglas, or some other sturdy material. The context for the work usually is described in a block of text at the beginning of the panel, with photos of the work process following, together with explanatory notes and samples of children's work and dialogue. As with all

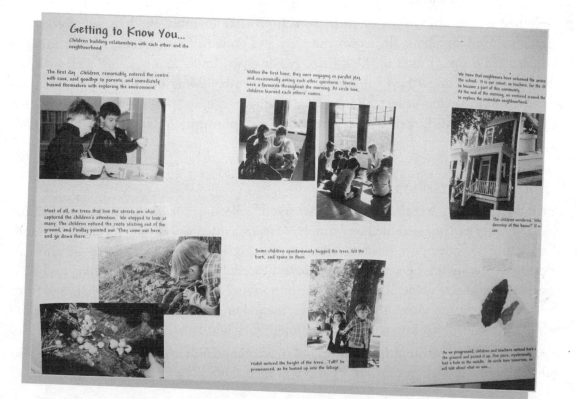

documentation, we try to make visible to others the meaning of what is happening, the learning that is taking place, and both the child's voice and the teacher's voice. Documentation panels make for fascinating reading. When well presented, they invite everyone in the school to stop for a while to read and therefore to understand.

All of the previously described options for preserving traces of children's work are useful in constructing documentation panels. If children consent to leaving their sculptures or models at school awhile, these can be placed directly in front of the documentation panels. If they are light enough, they can be suspended overhead.

Classroom Books

During our days with children, we see them concentrating and working hard to represent their ideas through play. This process can be recorded for the children themselves to revisit, in the form of classroom books to be kept in all areas of the room. For instance, in one classroom, children had an idea for a zoo, negotiated over a period of days with others about how to build it in the block area, and finally represented their ideas with blocks and dialogue. A book containing photos and transcripts of dialogue from the building process makes the story of their work available to them. A book of this type can be created simply by assembling pages on which to mount both photographs and some dictation from children, and then stapling pages together for children to read in the area where the play occurred or for long-term use in the book area.

When they're able to revisit their work from time to time, children will sometimes engage in thinking about their own thinking and growth. For instance, it's not unusual to hear a child say, "I used to think that . . . but now I know that . . ." or "That's when I was little! Now I know how to do that." Also, when reviewing documentation, children pay attention to what other children are thinking and doing. This tendency, combined with engagement with their teachers, provides an opportunity for scaffolding each child's understanding.

Children's Portfolios

Portfolios provide one of the most efficient ways of collecting documentation for individual children. They can be assembled very simply, by using a three-ring binder for each child and, after careful consideration, placing various artifacts inside over the long term—a semester or perhaps a year. Teachers and children reflect carefully upon what to include, and why. Possible questions may include: What is the importance of this artifact for the child or from the teachers' point of view? Is there a developmental message here? An avid interest on the part of the child? Learning made visible through the child's play or representations?

Although there are multiple approaches to creating children's portfolios, there are also some common threads in terms of what might be included:

- Samples of the child's work: drawings, writing in its many developmental forms, paintings, and photos of sculptures and models.

- Anecdotes that show both the child's ideas and the teacher's thinking, thereby supporting the reader's understanding of what happened.

- Narratives that describe in detail a particular event.

- Photos of the child in the process of exploration and during play.

- Transcripts of dialogue among children and between teachers and the child.

- A place for parents to record their thoughts, questions, and responses.

- A copy of the curriculum path, reduced on a photocopier to fit, so that parents can see the big picture of a particular project.

Such a rich collection of the child's work provides a meaningful starting point for discussions between parents and teachers. For instance, you may comment, "This is what your child did and this is what we understand from that," or "This is what your child learned, and this is how we know," or "This is what the whole class has been investigating, and this is your child's role." Because they're responding to concrete evidence of their child's work and play, parents frequently have lots to say about a portfolio. And always, they are delighted to see such a thoughtful and thorough record of their child's time at school.

Organizing Space and Time

Producing meaningful documentation clearly takes organization—not only of observations, photographs, and artifacts, but also of time and physical space. You will need a place to keep what you collect and space in which to assemble and construct. And then you, or someone who is supporting you, needs the time to put it all together.

Although space is usually at a premium in early childhood settings, collecting pieces of documentation needn't take too much space if you are well organized. Sometimes you only need to look at existing space with new eyes:

- Is there a shelf top in your classroom where clutter seems to collect? We all have them! If you clear the clutter, there may well be room for efficiently storing holding files (see the photograph on page 40). Note in this photo the simple and inexpensive wire holder. Paper documentation of any kind can be popped into folders, as long as they're emptied on a regular basis. Decisions need to be made here: What could go in the child's portfolio? What could be considered for documentation? What can be sent home?

- Do you have a staff room or a storage closet? If you're committed to collecting artifacts for documentation, a shelf or a portion of a cupboard could serve as your collection point. Even a cardboard file box at the bottom of a closet can effectively hold items for the short term, but you must have a system for examining file folders and making decisions. Does this need to be done weekly? Biweekly? Who will be responsible for this?

In cramped settings or in borrowed spaces with no built-in storage areas, you need to be brutal about cleaning up clutter and sorting through collections in a timely manner. There simply is no space for holding huge collections for the long term.

Another challenge is keeping documentation panels or logs as a school archive. Some schools find spaces in their attics or basements for this, and others use technology to store documentation for the long term. Rather than keeping a whole series of panels, for instance, they can be photographed, stored on a CD or flash drive, and will then be protected and saved for the long term using little physical space.

For early childhood education professionals, time also seems to be forever in short supply. In order for documentation to happen, there has to be support for teachers, who are busy with children in their classrooms, with meeting parents and each other, or with gathering resources. How can documentation be pulled together and presented?

If your organization can afford a substitute teacher for just an hour a week, a classroom teacher could then leave the room to concentrate on documentation. Teachers who engage in this type of work often find it to be a wonderful learning experience. When considering documentation, teachers must make decisions about what to use and why, and how to make thinking and learning visible. Wrestling with such decisions can help teachers grow in the areas of interpretation, connections to theory, and putting theory into practice. When administrators view documentation as a professional development opportunity, funds to support it sometimes can be made available.

In some cases, a director who's provided with the raw data can put the documentation together in a way that the team feels is appropriate. Or a director might take a teacher's place in the classroom for an hour to allow the teacher to work on documentation. Some directors, even though they're tremendously busy, commit to carving out time on a regular basis to support staff in this way. They then reap the benefits of enhanced professional development as well as communication with parents and student teachers.

Perhaps you are lucky enough to have the gift of a parent volunteer, a student teacher or work-study student, an interested grandparent, or some other resource person. Bearing in mind that the teaching team has to decide what will appear in the documentation and write the text to go along with it, a volunteer can certainly paste it up after receiving some guidance and basic design techniques. Such an arrangement has the added benefit of creating further understanding of what is occurring in the classroom and why for the volunteer, as well the chance to be an important part of classroom life.

If neither time nor help is available, then at the very least, teachers who want to produce documentation on their own time need to be supplied with the tools they need to create documentation (see sidebar on page 120). In such situations, starting small is just fine. Even pairing a brief handwritten anecdote with a photograph and including your own thinking is a good first step.

Useful Tools for Creating Documentation Panels

- Sturdy paper, cardboard, or foam board on which to mount photographs and drawings

- Digital photos printed out on photo paper (or good-quality bond)

- Glue stick or adhesive spray (the latter can have toxic fumes; use it only in a well-ventilated area where children are not present)

- Square edge and ruler to ensure that everything mounted is level and square

- Cutting tools: large scissors, a cutting blade, or a paper cutter

- Hanging materials: blu-tack or a similar product will protect walls; alternatively, use a cable system for hanging documentation with clips, or use a cord or wire across a wall or window for attaching photos or panels

- Small clips or clothespins if photos are to be hung rather than permanently attached

- Pertinent samples of children's graphic art, or artifacts they have made or collected (these can be attached with a hot-glue gun, or placed in front of documentation on a shelf)

Documentation and Early Childhood Education Learning Standards

In your setting, are you required to connect your documentation to particular learning standards set by a higher authority? This is becoming a more common practice in early childhood education. For example, Head Start settings have very specific standards that they must meet and document on a regular basis. Many states and provinces have developed Early Learning Guidelines, and although these are not always mandated for use in early childhood education classrooms, they are certainly highly recommended as a baseline for quality early childhood practices. Some centers have adopted Developmentally Appropriate Practice as their guide, and use the National Association for the Education

of Young Children (NAEYC) publication of the same name as a resource for their classrooms and teaching practice. Still others have checklists for learning outcomes that have been developed by their own organization.

How does a teacher in a play-based classroom that generates emergent curriculum connect children's investigations, play, ideas, and representations to standards and outcomes? Be reassured that we teachers know that all types of learning are taking place in our classrooms; we simply have to recognize them, name them, and make them visible. Consider the following examples:

Several four- and five-year-olds are gathered at a table with drawing materials. John, who is attempting to draw a starfish, says he needs new paper because he "messed up." Kenny tells him, "No, see . . . if you just make two lines like a V, you've made one. See, you did it. Just ask me for help if you want it."

What can we say about the prior knowledge and learning taking place here? Using the language of assessment, we might say:

- John attempts to make graphic representations of his ideas.

- Kenny is aware of other children around him, and he is able to share his own knowledge to assist them as needed.

- Kenny shows spatial awareness; he can connect his knowledge of letter forms to other situations such as drawing.

Three-year-old Sonya is at the writing table. She has chosen thin strips of white paper from the nearby shelves and has produced zigzags on one, circles on another, and undulating lines across a third. Taking another strip, she writes her name (spelled correctly). She consistently writes from left to right. Then she tapes her thin strips of paper together so they run like lines on a page from top to bottom. Sonya says, "I'm writing these because I wanted it to be beautiful for my momma. I made Os on that one. I like to write letters. My momma taught me. I like to tape things together."

We can see that there is much prior knowledge here; let's try to describe it:

- Sonya shows an interest in writing; she independently chooses writing materials during play.

- Sonya shows an understanding of the mechanics of print. She writes from left to write, and she organizes her print from top to bottom.

- Sonya produces both recognizable letters and letterlike forms. For instance, she refers to her circles as *Os*.

So, in a well-provisioned and engaging classroom, the learning is present and we can describe it. Now, it needs to be organized in a way that allows administrators, parents, and colleagues to see it. In the United States and Canada, I have encountered three common types of required processes for describing learning, although there are sure to be others. Let's consider the possibilities from the perspectives of these three types of requirements: programs that are required to use specified learning outcomes, programs that use a specific vocabulary for describing experiences, and programs that do not have to use a specified format but in which teachers write progress notes for parents.

Programs with Specific Learning Outcomes

Some programs choose to use specific materials developed by others to guide their expectations for young children. For instance, a kindergarten program may choose to use the National Council of Teachers of Mathematics (NCTM) Principles and Standards for School Mathematics. In the expectations for grade pre-K to two, one criterion is for children to "Connect number words and numerals to the quantities they represent, using various physical models and representations" (Copley and NAEYC 2000, 177).

How is this expectation met within the emergent curriculum, play-based program? Quite simply, by providing appropriate materials and the opportunity for children to represent what they know, along with the presence of a keen observer as children use the materials. Here's one such observation.

On a table near the block area, five-year-old Ali has set up the zoo animals in a long line. Another child comments, "Wow! You have hundreds!" Ali thinks for a moment before responding, "No, not *that* many!" From a nearby shelf, she takes some cubes with numerals imprinted on them and places them in order alongside the animals. As she puts them in order, she says each number aloud. Finishing, she tells her friend, "See! There are seventeen!" She then writes the numeral *17* on a small card and leaves it on the table next to the animals.

Programs with a Specific Vocabulary

Bob, a student whose practicum placement is in a High/Scope classroom, is learning the vocabulary associated with that learning environment. This includes Key Experiences, which describe "what young children do, how they perceive their world, and the kinds of experiences that are important for their development" (Hohmann and Weikart 1995, 297). One of his assignments is to observe play, collect anecdotes about the young children in his classroom, and then organize them under the headings of Key Experiences. The binders Bob has set up for children therefore have separate pages for each key experience: Creative Representation, Language and Literacy, Initiative and Social Relations, Movement, Music,

Classification, Seriation, Number, Space and Time. Had Bob been part of the earlier example with John and Kenny, he might have chosen to place the information about John in Creative Representation, and the information about Kenny in the areas of Social Relations, Space, and Language and Literacy.

Programs Where Teachers Write Progress Notes

Ann, who works in a center that uses emergent curriculum but no formal assessment techniques or checklists, is required to write progress notes about each child twice a year. She gives one copy of her notes to parents and places another copy in the child's portfolio. When she meets with parents to discuss a portfolio, the progress notes provide a concise but detailed summary of the child's development. At this center, the progress notes are broken down into learning domains: language, literacy, representation, logic and math, creativity, gross-motor, and fine-motor. Under each heading, Ann not only describes where the child is developmentally in terms of the domain but also connects her comments to the artifacts present in the portfolio. The artifacts help her remember everything the child has been doing. Here is one excerpt from a progress note:

Creativity: Martin consistently demonstrates his ability to think creatively. For instance, when other children encounter difficulties while building in the block area, Martin often thinks of a different approach using novel materials. He is also enthusiastic about creative movement, and during circle time frequently offers suggestions for new ways to move to music. His creative representations at the easel are full of wild creatures and adventures!

All of these examples demonstrate that children's activities, learning, ideas, and development can be made visible and described in many ways. If your organization requires that you use the formal language of assessment, you can use that language and your documentation of children's work within emergent curriculum to show children's learning and progress. If you are free to decide which form of assessment and accountability to use, then documentation offers you an opportunity to show exactly what is happening, and why.

The Teacher's Voice: Old Tree

At Ralph Waldo Emerson School for Preschoolers, the beloved old white pine that stood right outside the playroom window—the tree everybody in the school knew as Old Tree— was showing signs of its age. After a storm brought down several branches on the roof, the groundskeeper worried about safety. The teachers agonized over having Old Tree removed, for the tree was an integral part of the life of the school. Since the school's beginning, children had watched through the window or from outdoors as Old Tree changed through the seasons, provided a home to birds and squirrels, and offered shelter for them as they played outside under a hot sun. Though the children and staff loved Old Tree, it had to go. After deciding to make saying good-bye to the tree the focus of their work with the children, the teachers chose to document their attachment to Old Tree, the children's perceptions of the tree itself, and its eventual removal.

Director Susan Hagner wanted to capture not only Old Tree but its deeper, more personal connection to the children. How could the teachers show this? How could she and the teachers prepare the children for such a momentous and sad event as Old Tree being cut down?

Susan describes her thoughts as the teachers approached this investigation.

> The day we learned our big old tree had to come down, we began having conversations about the tree at gathering time. Getting the news was upsetting. And we had very little time to prepare the children, for Old Tree was to come down in only three weeks. The teachers were emotional, and the children wanted to understand our feelings too. We began our work by documenting conversations. Here is a sample of the text from our documentation.

OLD TREE

The day we learned our big old tree had to come down, children and teachers began to have conversations about the tree at circle time.

The grounds-keeper of the church, Barbara, said the tree is very old. Matthew guessed 7 years, Timmy guessed 109 years, River guessed 30 years and Lillian guessed 14 years.

Barbara also told us the tree is leaning towards the building and Lillian thought maybe we could push it up with our hands to keep it from falling, Timmy said we should use two big sticks to help hold it up… But old tree is 125 feet tall and won't be able to stand up against strong winds, as it gets even older.

We decided to take some walks around old tree. Matthew noticed old tree is taller than the tree on the other side of the building. When standing at the base of old tree we looked up and saw all the branches coming out. A nest exclaims Timmy. We also noticed how branches from other trees touch the branches of old tree. We looked closely at the bark and noticed the deep cracks and insect holes.

Then we decided to hug old tree. It took seven children to hug all the way around!

Back at circle we asked the children if trees have feelings. Yes. A tree will feel sad if it gets cut down. Trees will cry or they will break down. All the other trees will get really sad when old tree gets cut down. But maybe we could take pictures to remember old tree. And maybe we could save pieces of old tree for the playground or maybe build something… We could build another tree fort with a wooden slide to get down and a ladder to get up… Maybe make stepping circles… We should count the rings to find out how old the tree is.

We'll miss old tree but through pictures and stories we will remember old tree for always.

The groundskeeper told the children the tree is very old. Matthew guessed seven years, Timmy guessed a hundred and nine years, River guessed thirty years, and Lillian guessed fourteen years. We were also informed that the tree was leaning towards the building. Lillian thought maybe we could push it up with our hands to keep it from falling. Timmy said to use two big sticks to help hold it up. But we learned Old Tree was 125 feet tall and wouldn't be able to stand up against strong winds as it got even older.

We decided to take some walks around Old Tree. Matthew noticed Old Tree is taller than the tree on the other side of the building. While standing at the base of Old Tree we looked up and saw all the branches coming out. "A nest!" exclaimed Timmy. We also noticed how branches from other trees were touching the branches of Old Tree. We looked closely at the bark and noticed the deep cracks and insect holes. Then we decided to hug Old Tree. It took seven children to hug all the way around!

When, back at gathering time, we asked the children if trees have feelings, they said:

Yes. A tree will feel sad if it gets cut down.

Trees will cry or they will break down.

All the other trees will get really sad when Old Tree gets cut down.

Maybe we could take pictures to remember Old Tree.

And maybe we could save pieces of Old Tree for the playground or maybe to build something.

We could build another tree fort with a wooden slide to get down and a ladder to get up.

Maybe we could make stepping circles.

We could count the rings to find out how old the tree is.

The text for this documentation sets the scene for the reader. It puts the photos and drawings in context, explains the emotions attached to the tree, and describes why the teachers wanted to document the children's dialogue about the tree. From reading this text, it is clear that Old Tree is important to both children and teachers. The text reveals what the children's ideas are about saving the tree, about what the tree might feel, and about what might be done when the inevitable happens and the tree comes down.

Reading this documentation, we get a sense of the emotional life of the school, the respect shown for children's ideas and feelings, and the collaboration between teachers and children.

Throughout the next few weeks, children had many opportunities to study the tree and to represent it. One interesting aspect of their drawings and paintings was that many children represented only the trunk. After reflection, the teachers realized that for the children, this is the part of the tree that they were able to see close up, and touch. In other words, the trunk was what they had been able to directly experience—it was personal.

Here, we see how important it is for teachers to consider the artifacts—in this case, the drawings—they have collected. It was a small thing to notice that the children often drew only the trunk of the tree; it was insightful to realize—after reflection—that this was the children's perspective and that it represented their direct experience.

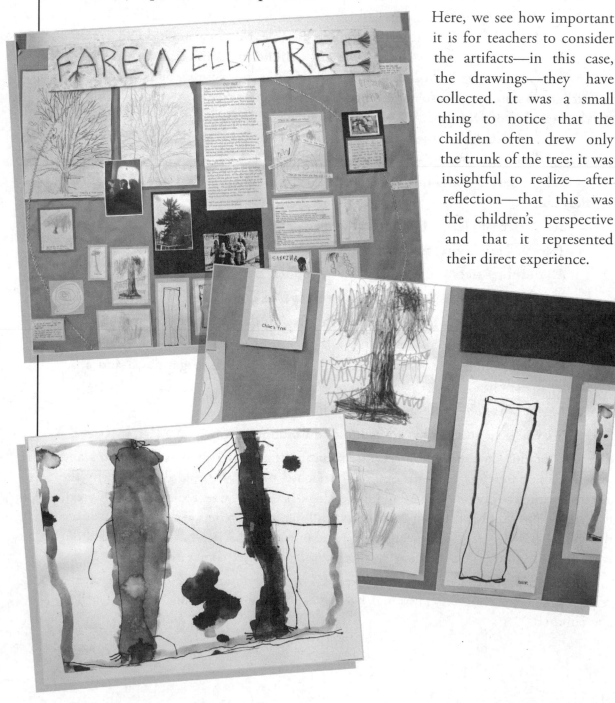

When tree-removal day arrived, the children watched, transfixed, as Old Tree came down branch by branch. Their feelings were acknowledged and validated. The whole process was carefully photographed. The children told us, "We'll miss Old Tree but with our pictures and stories we will remember its life."

These days, the children have three round cuts from Old Tree that serve as stepping-stones on the playground. The tree's bottom wedge is displayed prominently inside the school as a reminder of its size and grandeur. A huge tree stump outside the window is used as a feeder, and seed and fruit are placed there regularly so the children can watch as animals come and go. Old Tree continues to provide joy and learning for the children.

This documentation is meaningful on many levels. It validates the children's feelings and their relationship with Old Tree. They are able to revisit this documentation—it is displayed prominently in the room where they gather—and talk about it whenever they want. Making the documentation was an important process for both teachers and children. It enabled the teachers to open up conversations with children, to acknowledge what they knew about the tree as well as their feelings about it, and to think among themselves about what the children's representations told them. Finally, the documentation provided for parents and visitors a window into the world of a school that strives to create community and respect.

The Child's Voice: Collaborating with Teachers

If children's portfolios do indeed represent experiences and learning, then it makes sense that children will have some ideas about what might go into their portfolios.

At Jubilee Road Children's Center in Halifax—a brand-new child care center using emergent approaches—the children were first introduced to their portfolios during small-group time. Since the children had been attending the school only for about four days, most of the portfolios were empty.

The children recognized their names on the spine of each binder. They looked inside to find empty plastic sleeves. The teacher explained that these were their portfolios, and that they or the teachers could place some of their work inside to keep. The children decided that the binders needed pictures on the front—they were too plain. So, this small-group time was spent with the children drawing themselves, and then describing the things they liked to do while the teacher wrote their words. Most of the children wrote their own name on their self-portrait, which was attached to the front of their binder.

Over the next few days, some of the children began to show an intense interest in their portfolios. They looked inside each day to see if anything new had appeared, and they themselves placed drawings and writing inside. On those occasions, the teachers asked the children to talk a little about their work and then included these notes with the artifact.

Here are some examples of the children's first responses to seeing their portfolios on the classroom shelf:

I know which is mine; it has my name.

My stuff is in here—there's my writing!

I played Scrabble, and then I wrote the words.

Look! [to another child] Here's my work!

There are lots of empty pages.

Susan, when can I put more things in here?

Can I take this home?

Keeping the children's work in a special place that is theirs creates both pride in their work and interest in what happens next. From time to time, we hear children say—almost to themselves—"I'm going to put this in my portfolio." When full, the portfolios will indeed go home to be kept by parents as a precious record of their child's preschool years. But while the portfolios remain at the center, the children themselves treasure them, and peruse both their own and others' on a regular basis.

Suggested Readings

Gronlund, G., and B. Engel. 2001. *Focused Portfolios: A Complete Assessment for the Young Child.* St. Paul: Redleaf Press.

The President and Fellows of Harvard College on Behalf of Project Zero. 2003. *Making Teaching Visible: Documenting Individual and Group Learning as Professional Development.* Cambridge, Mass.: Project Zero.

7

The Teacher as Researcher

Children are the ultimate researchers, for they are finding out how the world works. To do this, they engage in experiences with their minds and bodies, experiment using trial and error, ask questions, watch others carefully and imitate their actions, and attentively watch life unfold. Children have theories about how things work, and they are not afraid to take a stab at even the most complex puzzles: How does a photocopier work? How do airplanes get up in the air? Asked these questions, an adult might say, "I haven't a clue!" But four- or five-year-olds will often make an attempt to think such things through, and their insightful answers will surprise us. We just have to ask.

Early childhood educators who work directly with children in the classroom might hesitate to call themselves researchers. Yet, if we think of research as a way of being in the classroom, a process of investigating and studying in order to reach new conclusions, then we can see that early childhood educators who use an emergent approach to curriculum are also researchers. In this type of practice, we are immersed in data all day long. If we are paying attention to it, recording it, and using it in order to develop new understandings and approaches, then we are engaged in a cycle of inquiry.

Teacher research is based in this cycle of inquiry, with the teacher taking on a questioning disposition. What does the teacher question? For a reflective practitioner, just about everything is food for thought. As presented by Jeanne Goldhaber and Dee Smith at the University of Vermont, the cycle of inquiry begins with formulating a question. As you work in the classroom, everything that you observe, record, and collect becomes data that can be organized and then analyzed and interpreted. From this analysis, which usually is undertaken in dialogue with colleagues, one can begin to form theories about what is happening, what the children are thinking about, and what the possibilities might be for future work. Inevitably, even more questions arise from this process, leading one to observe again (in Hill, Stremmel, and Fu 2005). Thus, we become engaged in a cyclical, ongoing process that deepens our understandings of, and collaborations with, children.

Susan Hagner, director at Emerson Preschool, describes what this looks and feels like for her team:

> We are like scientists researching what children are interested in. . . .We're gathering data, and through the pictures that we take and the notes that we write, we make decisions about what's happening. In our weekly or daily meetings, I bring this data, and it triggers memories for us, it gives us discussion points. I think photography has really changed things. For me, it triggers memories that I haven't written down. There are threads that happen every day, but you don't necessarily link them until you look back over six weeks of photographs and notes and think "That's where this all started!"

As Susan points out, sometimes we don't immediately understand the meaning of what we have seen, but in looking back over time, meaning becomes clearer. Inquiry is not usually linear, with a tidy beginning and end, but rather is circular or spiral or meandering in its progress. In other words, we move forward a little with what we think we understand, and then revisit that hypothesis when we learn more as a result of continued observation and reflection about children's ongoing work and developing ideas.

Reflection and teacher research are intertwined; one needs to think deeply in order to find answers, or even to make decisions about what to do next in order to find those answers. Lawre Goodnow, a preschool teacher in New Hampshire, comments, "I think about how important the master class (Emergent Curriculum Collaborative) was for me, because the issues we discussed there were deeper and broader in scope than they ever were in the classroom context. It was these deeper questions (Why do children build houses? Enclosures? What are the children looking for when they pretend to be pets?) that elevated the mindset that I brought to the classroom. Thinking about these questions allowed me to be more observant and less hurried to 'do something,' to teach, to intervene, to interrupt. Reflection allowed me the opportunity to stretch time. I worried less about how my invitation was affecting the play, and more about what the play was."

When Lawre mentions the idea of "stretching time," she echoes the need that most teachers experience: we simply don't have time to stop and think deeply about what's happening when we are in the middle of it. Yet when we do find time outside of the classroom to sit back and think—especially with colleagues—we begin to find questions that we are interested in pursuing. The question might be as big as "How do children show us their thinking?" or "How do children scaffold each others' learning?" On the other hand, you may wonder about something quite specific or practical, such as "How does our daily routine improve or restrict the flow of play?" or "Why do the children insist upon moving blocks around the room?"

Every teacher's practice and philosophy will differ from that of other teachers in some ways and be similar in others. The excitement in teacher research is that no matter what curricula you have used or how you have been trained, you will always have questions about what children are doing, why and how they are doing it, and what you as a teacher can learn from that. In other words, as a curious educator, you will always have "burning questions."

Guidelines for Teacher Research

There are many types of teacher research, and several ways of entering the process. In fact, whole books are dedicated to this topic. But for the purpose of drawing together all the aspects of emergent curriculum that we have discussed in this book, I will make connections between the elements of emergent curriculum and some general guidelines for teacher research.

Formulate Your Question

Earlier, we learned about how and what to observe, how to record those observations, and how to organize them so they can be discussed later and perhaps used for curriculum planning purposes. If you have done this much, you are in a strong position to formulate questions for teacher research, which is the beginning of the inquiry cycle.

As you read through your notes and look at photographs and artifacts, many questions are likely to arise. If there are too many questions, you must narrow them down to make the work manageable, or else find a focus that your teaching team is interested in pursuing as a group. Or you can certainly conduct teacher research as an individual, with colleagues playing a supportive role.

When developing one of your burning questions, you may find the following points helpful:

- What puzzles you about what you've observed or heard in the classroom? What intrigues you to the point that you'd like to learn more? What do you wonder?

- What causes disequilibrium for you? Sometimes we observe play or hear dialogue from children that challenges our previous understandings. Follow this discomfort—it can lead to new learning about yourself and your practices.

- Think about the phrasing of your question. Is your question answerable through data collection? Will you be able to answer your question through observation, invitations, dialogue, reading, or revisiting documentation?

- Remember that teacher research should inform your teaching. You will no doubt use previous experiences, knowledge, and training to help you uncover answers and deepen your understanding, but whatever your question is, researching it should affect what you do in the classroom and how you do it.

- Can you involve others in formulating theories in response to your question? The children? Other teachers? Parents? The community?

Collaboration and Support

Under ideal circumstances, emergent curriculum involves thinking with others. During your planning meetings or in conversation with peers or your supervisor, you might wish to raise your research question, share your initial observations, and see if there is someone who wishes to collaborate with you. If there is, two heads are generally better than one, but if there isn't, you can certainly ask others to take on a supporting role, "keep their eyes open" for events, take notes, and collect artifacts that may be useful to you. Also, your administrator can be a huge support, by providing encouragement, resources, and that most precious commodity, time.

What other supports do you need? Perhaps professional literature will be useful, or a workshop or seminar. Sometimes a conversation with a knowledgeable colleague can be extremely helpful. Do you have families who might be interested in thinking with you? Perhaps the families of the involved children would like to at least follow what you are thinking about. If invited, some may contribute their own insights.

Review and Reflect

Examining your data (observations, photographs, artifacts, etc.) has to be an ongoing process. Sometimes, in order to pull out meaning from what we are seeing and to find answers to our questions, we have to look again. Doing so allows you to reflect on what particular data is telling you, what the possibilities for future action might be, or what further questions the data brings to mind. Collaboration at this point is desirable, since what we cannot see alone often becomes clearer when we discuss it with others. Many perspectives also give you food for further thought.

Develop Hypotheses

This may sound very scientific, but it's actually quite simple. What are your ideas or theories about what is happening in the classroom? Trust yourself to make an educated guess. You are trying to inform your own teaching, so that as curriculum develops, you will begin to have ideas about how and why things are happening in a particular way. As you analyze your data, you are attempting to make meaning out of what you have seen. Practice doesn't always have to come from theory; theories can also come from your practice.

Reflection is essential at this point, as is taking one's time. That's why video and audio recordings are so useful; they stop time in order for us to examine events more closely. As you reflect, and as you engage in professional dialogue, you will almost certainly find yourself developing theories about what is happening. As these theories begin to build, perhaps quite tentatively, you will be able to think about strategies that will enable you to respond to children (such as scaffolding, providing invitations, engaging in long-term projects, or making changes to the environment).

In addition, you can be thinking about how your theories may affect your future teaching. Thus, curriculum emerges and theories develop side by side. Children's theories and teacher's theories are each respected as teacher and child collaborate and move forward in the learning journey. Both teacher and child are learners; both are researchers.

Plan Next Steps

Here's where we spiral back to the beginning of the cycle. As you plan what to do next (responding both to children and to your own questions and theories), you once again begin the cycle of inquiry: observing and documenting, reflecting and collaborating, theory building and responding. When you are in a questioning frame of mind, it's not at all unusual to arrive back at the beginning of the cycle with more questions than before. Rather than thinking of this as a setback, think instead of the growth that's occurring when teachers have more questions than answers!

In the following example, a series of questions occur to preschool teacher Katie as she watches children carefully and not only wonders about what they're doing but why no representational work is occurring.

The Teacher's Voice: Katie's Burning Question

Complex block building had long been an interest of the children at CFDC. A major part of the classroom curriculum had been developed in response to this, with scaffolding and documentation taking place over several weeks. Katie, who was again carefully watching this play, invited the children to represent their structures graphically.

This preschool team had long held the belief that when children use various media to represent their work, it helps to solidify their knowledge and stretch their thinking. In Dr. George Forman's *Jed Draws His Bicycle* video, he makes the point that a child's thinking can be challenged and scaffolded when the child is invited to think through and show how something works. Thinking similarly, Katie had often invited the children to draw their structures. The reply from these very competent four- and five-year-olds was always the same: "I can't draw." In addition, most of the boys in the classroom refused to have anything to do with the art studio, no matter how inviting and stimulating the materials might be.

As a team, the teachers discussed the children's perception that they couldn't draw. When I met with the team, we remembered together how drawing used to be a part of play and home life when we were children. To keep us occupied, our own parents often just provided us with pencils and paper and left us to our own devices. We hypothesized that perhaps TV or computers were now used to keep children occupied when parents were busy. In any case, Katie saw that there was an opportunity to build children's confidence in this area, and she set about devising some small-group times to achieve this. Her burning questions were "How can I connect the children's intense interest in block building with representing this work in various ways in the art studio?" and "How can I build confidence in drawing?"

At this point, we can see that Katie has been observing carefully. She has noticed—in addition to the children's play—an unwillingness to draw, and she wonders about this. As a curious practitioner, she not only asks why but also confers with her team members, who together consider their values, their prior knowledge, and what might happen next.

In the fall, Katie offered small-group times with just a half-dozen blocks for each child. In order to take a step back and begin in the developmental space inhabited by the children, Katie devised a copycat game wherein one child would form a design with the blocks and the others would attempt to reproduce it. The children adored this game and wanted to play it over and over again. This very concrete form of representation, Katie hypothesized, developed the children's ability to see the components of a block design.

Then, Katie offered different materials with which children could represent their buildings. She first tried Lego blocks, but this proved to be challenging. The children perceived that Legos had to be used vertically and that they couldn't represent their horizontal designs with them. It didn't occur to them to use the Legos differently. One child even changed his block building to a vertical design so he could more successfully represent it with Legos!

After reconsidering, Katie offered a different set of materials. She chose two-dimensional materials including small foam shapes and popsicle sticks, because these, she reasoned, mimicked the shapes of their unit blocks, but on a smaller scale. The children were very successful with this form of representation. Using these new materials, they could look at a simple block structure and represent it flat on the floor, or by using glue on paper. This important shift, from three-dimensional to two-dimensional re-representation, provided a huge leap in the children's ability to see things from different perspectives.

It's important to note here that Katie has been carefully considering what the children can do, what they cannot do, and what she can do to scaffold. She offers not one invitation, but several, until the children seem to feel more comfortable. She is also keeping the work both playful and tied into their interest in block building, while introducing the idea of re-representation.

After the children had worked with these materials on a regular basis for two or three weeks, Katie again invited them to represent what they had done—with paint. Several children attempted this and were satisfied with the results. Since the block structures they

were creating at small-group time were much simpler than those they'd created in the block area, and since they had now had some experience with two-dimensional representation, the children were less intimidated by graphic representation.

Now that the children were representing during small-group activities, Katie once more offered the opportunity to draw more complex buildings in the block area. This time, she noticed both more confidence and a level of finesse in their drawings.

What did Katie learn from pursuing the answer to her questions? Here is an excerpt from a conversation I had with her:

SUSAN: What have you learned from doing this?

KATIE: A few children could picture in their mind and then draw, but for most, this was a struggle. This struggle, and my feeling that they were a little afraid of drawing, led me to try to help them be successful with using varied media. How could I make it easier? It was hard thinking; What could I do to enable the children to be successful at this? The varied media—Popsicle sticks, flat foam shapes—mimicked the blocks they were using; they were similar in that they were kind of flat. I had to learn to watch the struggles, rethink the materials, and take a step back to simpler drawings of four-block structures.

SUSAN: So there was a period of reevaluating?

KATIE: Yes—hard thinking! And I need to look at things like this repeatedly, maybe every six months, to look for growth. I was really surprised at their development. They eventually went from not drawing at all to representing buildings using a pencil.

SUSAN: What do you think were your influences on the children throughout this process?

KATIE: One of the things I did recently, just to see if they could do it, was to ask them to draw a plan first and then build . . .

SUSAN: So, you were flipping the process, turning it around to use drawing differently . . .

KATIE: Yes, and I had to scaffold this. When they were stuck, I invited them to think about the shapes within the block buildings, and this got them started and I could retreat again.

SUSAN: How has this changed your approach to teaching?

KATIE: We have always taught from our observations here. These are experienced block builders, but I had to think about what they can do and what they can't do, and if they can't do something, I need to step back and think about it, and offer new challenges so they can move forward. We can really scaffold representation more; it's something we haven't done a lot of—our studio area is very open ended. But we can teach them how to use materials and tools . . . all the usual choices would be available, but the teachers could offer more opportunities to represent objects that are of interest to the children, and if done on a daily basis, this could be relaxing, and build confidence. I think in society there is some fear of drawing—I know there is for me!—and we have to take the fear out.

Katie's hard thinking is evident throughout her work. From this conversation, we get a sense of the curiosity, care, and thought that went into her offerings to the children. The children's growth provoked her to think about what they could and could not do and to carefully scaffold in response to that. Katie now has in mind a plan for how studio work in this classroom might be fine-tuned, a plan that is based on what she's learned from the children.

Following her research, Katie did in fact start offering familiar and interesting found materials in the art area on a regular basis, as an invitation to draw. And the children did become happily engaged with drawing. They also had lots to say about their drawings, which in turn made their thinking more visible to the teachers. The children now had the confidence to use the language of graphic representation on a regular basis and for many different purposes.

We see that Katie had a beginning curiosity, formed a question, drew upon many observations and artifacts, and then had the opportunity to take her time to think about this puzzle and to engage in dialogue with others. Finally, she planned a response to the children and documented what happened, and then she observed again. Throughout this cycle, Katie was learning about herself and about teaching—especially in the area of scaffolding—as she became deeply engaged on an intellectual level with the work.

The Child's Voice: Children as Researchers

A preschool child once said to me, "My mom is home doing research," and I asked, "Do you know what that is, research?" He replied, "Research is finding out about stuff." How simple, and how exact. Teachers and children both want to find out about stuff. Sometimes teachers and children can research together—for instance, when the topic is unfamiliar to both. And sometimes, when the children show an interest in something the teacher knows about, she chooses to let the children uncover it for themselves. While they do, she supports them with resources and experiences that empower them in constructing their own knowledge.

The following anecdotes represent a few simple ways that teachers enabled children to build knowledge about their immediate community. The children at the brand-new Jubilee Road Children's Center in Halifax were from the immediate community, but they were new to each other, the teachers, and the building itself. The playroom afforded a wonderful view of a busy intersection, and during the first weeks of school, it was the traffic and the people in front of the house that engaged the children.

As the children watched the traffic go by, day after day, the teachers observed that they discriminated between the many types of trucks and cars and were particularly interested in counting taxicabs. The teachers wondered, "Why taxis? What are their previous experiences with taxis?" Reflecting on what exactly it was that interested the children, they decided it was probably both the lights on top—something the children always mentioned—and the sheer number of cabs that fascinated them. They seemed to find the number of cabs hilarious; as the number grew higher and higher each morning, the laughter would become uproarious. As an invitation, the teachers provided clipboards so the children could tally the cabs as they went by.

This engaged them for several days, until they noticed the guard at the crosswalk. The following comments were noted:

He holds up the stop sign and all the cars stop.

Everybody has to wait so they will be safe.

He brings his bike to work. It's tied to the pole!

Why doesn't he wave to us?

Soon afterward, another event fascinated the children: work on the chimney of a house across the street. Again, the children's dialogue provided some clues to their thinking:

Why is he wearing those straps?

He's shining his flashlight down the chimney. It must be broke.

He's putting something down there!

The teachers wondered how the children could research their own community, and how they could support that research. They decided that, as children noticed each aspect of this new-to-them environment, it would be photographed and revisited. They supplemented this documentation with regular neighborhood walks, which in turn led to the children pointing out the houses they knew, the bakery, the mail carrier, and so on. It soon became evident that some of the children knew the neighborhood in more detail than the teachers did. The teachers wondered if the children could show the teachers in graphic form where things are.

To answer this question (following a discussion with colleagues), a teacher presented at circle time the idea of mapping—beginning with the immediate school environment—with the hypothesis that this might spread to the whole neighborhood. The children were intensely interested in the map of the school. The teachers watched and waited. Soon, in the studio, one child spontaneously drew the whole neighborhood; other children then interacted with this map, talking about where they lived and where they'd been.

So, from the simple beginning of looking through a window at the community, teachers were able to reflect on what the children knew, give them the opportunity to show the teachers their neighborhood, create an invitation to represent this, and observe again. Children constructed their own knowledge of maps by representing what they knew; teachers answered their own questions about the children's abilities to represent their community, while at the same time building on the children's engagement with what they saw through the window.

Why Engage in Teacher Research?

Teachers' daily work with young children in the classroom is physically and mentally demanding, and the challenges are often compounded by being underpaid and undervalued by society. When teachers are overextended, it's extremely hard for them to keep passion in their work, especially if they aren't receiving positive feedback about what they do.

Perceiving yourself as a researcher provides a shift in thinking that transforms the everyday routines of the classroom into meaningful, intellectually stimulating, and rewarding work. Once you have made the shift in thinking about your classroom role, your understanding of what is happening in the classroom also begins to change.

Teachers become empowered, in that they are provoked to think deeply about their work, the meaning of teaching, and the thought processes of children. When we get to this—to asking "What is the child thinking? How can we make that visible? How can we demonstrate our work?"—then our curriculum belongs to the classroom and the wider community and takes on a life of its own. It becomes not what someone else thinks is "good for all children" but what is actually right for *this* group of children. The children and their families, the teachers and those who support them, all become engaged in the work. It gains the importance that it deserves, meanwhile fostering a love of learning in children, as well as in the teachers who love watching and supporting that process as it unfolds.

Suggested Readings

Ballenger, C. 1999. *Teaching Other People's Children: Literacy and Learning in a Bilingual Classroom.* New York: Teachers College Press.

Rinaldi, C. 2006. *In Dialogue with Reggio Emilia: Listening, Researching, and Learning.* New York: Routledge.

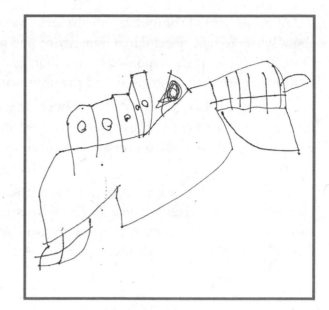

8

Putting It All Together

We have seen that for emergent curriculum to happen, several components need to be in place: observation in its many forms, followed by reflection and dialogue on the part of teachers, then thoughtful decision making, invitations for children, documentation of everything from ordinary moments to long-term projects, all leading to accountability. What do these many facets of emergent curriculum look like in real life as they come together to generate a full-bodied, rich curriculum that engages children and teachers? In answering that question, we will look at The Doll Project, which illustrates the delicate dance between children's play and teachers' responses. This exemplary long-term project was featured in an article in *Young Children* (Wien, Stacey, Keating, Rowlings, and Cameron 2002), parts of which are excerpted throughout this chapter.

The Doll Project was unusual in several respects. Although the children were very young—two to three years old—they remained engaged with the work over a period of months. This was astounding to both the teachers and parents, since we don't usually expect such long-term attention from children so young. In fact, some teachers hesitate to even attempt project work with younger children. Through examining this project, we will see that when teachers' responses are in tune with children's ideas and comments, even very young children can indeed maintain interest.

Also, the level of community involvement was unexpected, and the teachers' decisions about where to take the children were daring and novel. As the teachers became more and more creative in their responses to the children, the wider community wholeheartedly welcomed both the young group and the investigation they were part of.

This project also provides food for thought in terms of what kind of support is necessary for maintaining emergent curriculum. As this teaching team entered what was for them new territory, they received support from administration, from colleagues, from an artist, and from one another.

In following this project, then, we will see all aspects of emergent curriculum as they merge into an investigation: observation as a starting point; reflection among teachers and with administrators; invitations in the form of activities, materials, and field trips; and documentation to reflect upon and share.

This emergent curriculum began with a simple idea. The teachers noticed that the children were charmed by babies and frequently took out classroom dolls for washing, feeding, combing, carrying about, and putting to sleep. This play recurred over a period of weeks. After consultation and collaboration with others, the teachers decided to offer each child a handmade cloth doll without distinguishing features.

A network of relationships developed behind the scenes. Art consultant Rhonda Wakely-Fortin designed and constructed the dolls in a resplendent variety of skin tones and body shapes, from skinny mahogany to plump peach. She also devised simple shapes for facial features and hairpieces, which she enclosed in plastic zipper bags. Barb Bigelow, the center director, and Susan Stacey, the assistant director at the time, contacted Carol Anne Wien, who passed on ideas, books, and articles about the Reggio Emilia program in Italy and about emergent curriculum.

The director, with her interest in innovative practice, invited her staff to read portions of Edwards, Gandini, and Forman (1993) and to think about project work based on children's interests. Susan, who sat in on early planning meetings with the teachers, challenged their thinking, disseminated key readings, and prodded the teachers to begin the project. She also provided practical support for documentation (such as videotaping, taking photographs, getting photos developed), worked with the teachers to turn their documentation into finished panels for others to view, and transcribed conversations to be included with photographs and drawings in the teachers' portfolio system on individual children. But the project itself belonged to the teachers and the children.

The pedagogy of project work was new to the teachers. Susan, excited by Hendrick's (1997) descriptions of work with the ideas of Reggio Emilia, suggested starting with children's conversations. This seemed an unusual way to begin. Ideas from outside our culture often are strange to us and become interpreted, as we work with them, through the lens of our own cultural understandings; they are transformed as we process them within our range of experience.

As this project work begins, we can already see many aspects of emergent curriculum. The teachers began with observations of the children's play. It was ongoing and engaging, and in their opinion it warranted special attention. Then they consulted with others—their administration and the artist who eventually designed and constructed the dolls used for the project—and reflected on how to begin. Here, they were stepping into what was for them new territory. They started by taping conversations they had with the children so they could reflect on what the children said. Remember, nothing else had been planned in advance; it was these conversations that would lead the teachers. Anyone unfamiliar with this kind of approach might find it nebulous and somewhat intimidating. As we will see from the children's comments, however, if we are paying attention, the children will always point us toward the next step.

Thus it was with some trepidation that each teacher showed a small group of children a sample cloth doll and audiotaped their conversations.

"It's a baby. I have a baby."

"It has no eyes."

"I have a baby in my belly."

"Me too."

"It has no eyes, no lips, no teeth, no mouth, no hair either."

The Primacy of Eyes

The children, without exception, focused initially on the lack of eyes on the dolls. "My doll cannot see you," said David. Interesting! The teachers invited the children to study their own eyes using mirrors. One boy pulled down his eyelid saying, "Red eye. Look, Bobbi, red." Another said, "My eyes are brown in there," and someone else pointed out, "My eyes are white, Bobbi, see the white. There's black too. Let me see yours, Bobbi."

Together the teachers and children made a simple sorting chart on which each child placed two circles representing the color of his or her eyes. With mirrors close by, the children reexamined their dolls, discussing with the teachers what color their eyes should be. Then, using felt pieces of different colors from the plastic bags, they attached eyes to their dolls with fabric glue.

Joelle admits that she struggled hard "trying not to control" where children put the eyes on the dolls. The teachers used mirrors and talked about the eye placement in a factual way but did not challenge the children—"We just described back to them what they were doing." Three girls held their dolls up to the mirror, making them look at each other and talk. Aline said, "My doll has one blue eye and one green eye. She likes them like that."

The teachers made sure drawing paper and pencils were handy, and some children began drawing faces.

Since the doll's lack of eyes is clearly an interest, the teachers concentrate on ways for the children to explore their own. Mirrors and sorting charts help the children examine eyes more closely. If you are required to formally assess children's abilities, you might see here an opportunity to think about classification. Notice, however, that activities are set up not to evaluate what children know, but to respond to children's own ideas and to give them an opportunity to represent what they already know and may want to represent in various ways.

To further investigate and think about eyes, the teachers planned a visit to an optometrist's office. The children took along their dolls on the bus, holding them up to the windows and showing them things. They were very excited as they walked through the mall: many dolls developed weak necks because the children showed them things so vigorously.

At the optometrist's the children tried on glasses and sunglasses and talked about seeing. The teachers took photographs and gave the children drawing materials to record their reactions. Heather put glasses on two dolls, and the children looked at the dolls in amazement. Their comments:

"My mommy, my daddy—glasses."

"Beautiful!"

"They are holding from your ears, Joelle."

"My doll see a lot of things."

After the visit, the teachers expected the children might want to make glasses for their dolls. But Joelle reports, "Not one child said their doll needed glasses. We had to let it go. They enjoyed trying them on and putting them on the dolls, but that was enough."

There is an important stance on the part of the teachers here. They not only came up with a wonderful idea for a field trip but also knew when to let go of an idea that appealed only to them. Sometimes even the best ideas are of no interest to children. What we need to do is watch what really happens and respond to that.

Also, think about what went on behind the scenes in order for this field trip to happen. A teacher had to call around to find an optometrist's office willing to let a large group of young children visit, and then explain the reasoning behind this plan. It's important for teachers to be able to articulate to those outside our field not only what we are doing but why.

Overall the teachers were astonished at the amount of time the children were absorbed in examining and thinking and talking about eyes—not days, but weeks. When would their interest shift, and to what? Then the teachers heard children's comments, such as "My doll has no hair" and "My doll's head is cold." Such comments, in combination with the children's interest in combs and combing both their own and the teachers' hair, prompted the teachers to turn to hair.

Investigating Hair

The children were invited to accompany Heather when she went for a haircut at a local salon. The stylist was so pleased by the children's visit that she and her partner closed the shop for the morning so the children could explore the surroundings. The two- and three-year-olds tried out the chair that goes around and around and up and down, caught Heather's hair as it fell to the floor, and sat down and drew what they saw. The teachers took photographs and made documentation panels about the trip for the children to revisit. The group later made a book of photos, drawings, and children's comments as a thank-you gift for the salon staff.

A hairstylist was also invited to visit the classroom. Parents gave permission to snip a lock of each child's hair; some even gave permission for a full trim. Arthur was nervous before his turn, but after the first snip, he smiled and said, "Oh." The locks of hair were laminated on index cards labeled with each child's name on the back. The cards were assembled into a little book so the children could find their own hair and that of their friends and explore the different textures and colors.

Throughout the project, a classroom table was set aside as a place for investigating faces. There children could draw, look in mirrors, or experiment with changing features on their dolls. Now the teachers put out the hairpieces, which came in many colors, lengths, and textures. Some children matched their own hair; others wanted something different. The children arranged and glued hair as they saw fit. David commented, "Now he's a boy, 'cause he has short hair. I have short hair, and I'm a boy." One girl found a piece of string and wanted a ponytail for her doll. Suddenly many children wanted ponytails, and appropriate materials were provided at the project table.

Once again, we see unusual ideas from the teachers: a visit to a hair salon—not just to look, but to experience—and a haircutting session in the classroom. And we see the teachers finding ways for the children to hold onto their experiences so they can revisit them on an ongoing basis. Beginning with these two events, all the children's experiences throughout the project were documented on panels.

And where, exactly, were all these invitations and activities set up? As mentioned, there was a table where the investigation could continue through the use of intriguing materials; but where in the daily routine did this happen? When there is a table set up with materials, children can choose whether or not to participate during play. When the teacher has something more specific in mind, however, this activity can be accomplished during small-group time.

> In observing the play, the teachers noted that when they put a three-sided mirror on the playdough table, children began making faces—wrinkling noses, pulling on lips. Two children put playdough over their faces, making molds of their cheeks, noses, and lips. One child, pulling off the playdough mask, said, "See, that's my nose in there."
>
> The teachers extended this interest by having a college student with an arts background make a mask of Heather's face. When Heather's eyes were behind the mask, the children said good-bye and "We can't see you anymore." Heather thinks they realized that she could not see them, an interesting shift in perspective for the children.

What an unusual experience for children! And what did the children's responses tell the teachers? If you had been involved with this project, what kinds of scaffolding would you have provided in response to this shift in perspective?

> Soon the children pointed out that their dolls could not speak because they didn't have mouths.
>
> "Heather, my doll wants to kiss you but she has no lips."
>
> "My doll can't talk. Where's his mouth?"
>
> Such comments were cues for the teachers to move on.

Turning to Noses and Mouths

Since taste and smell are closely allied, the teachers decided to explore noses and mouths together. They planned many activities, including shopping trips; baking gingerbread people, bread, and pizza; and preparing fruit salad and homemade ice cream.

Susan took photos of the children's noses and mouths. These were displayed and the children were invited to find their own and their friends' noses and mouths. By this time the children were drawing faces repeatedly.

Bags of noses and mouths in different colors and shapes (long and skinny, round and full) were brought out, and the children chose the ones they wanted for their dolls and glued them on. Ian used his doll's nose for a belly button.

In many preschools, children explore noses and mouths during a preplanned focus on the senses. The difference between that approach and what we see here is that this focus has emerged from the children; it occurs in their time, in response to their interest. There is an organic feel about their arrival at this common preschool focus. And now that the children are ready, the teachers again provide interesting props and materials that build on previous work with the dolls.

A few children then complained that the dolls had no clothes: "My baby's cold." Rhonda, our doll maker, supplied simple clothes (dresses and pants) and many loose pieces of fabric (for sashes, bandanas, shawls, sarongs). The children dressed their dolls during small-group sessions.

"I put clothes on; she feels happy."

"Maybe there are skirts?"

"My dolly's name is Edward, and he's warm and he feels nice in his clothes."

"Girls have to have dresses because that's what they wear sometimes."

The children's drawings of people expanded exponentially. In April Julia's drawing of a woman was accompanied by an extended verbal description: "Round. Shoes here. That's her chin. Here's ears right here. There's a scarf, here we go. Nose, has nose. What else, Joelle? She has a ponytail on it. And has a button on it."

The teachers, we see, are still listening attentively to children's comments. As you follow the progress of this project, do you get a sense of the spiral that is evolving? Thinking back to the beginning of the project, in conversation the children noted the lack of eyes. Now they are noticing the lack of clothing, and, by listening again, the teachers know just what to do.

Making Beds for the Dolls

The children often put the dolls to bed, using anything at hand—a shelf, a scarf. The observant teachers planned a visit to a local hotel, where the children were invited to explore beds, taking a bed apart to see all the things used to make one up (bedspread, blanket, top sheet, bottom sheet, mattress pad). The children even investigated the box springs. They tried out the beds, getting in and out, and jumping on them (not a concern to the attendant). They also explored the contents of the hotel room. They climbed under the bed. One child said, "How does the mattress hold?" Children sat and drew what was interesting to them. One three-year-old chose to draw a flag visible out the window.

Rhonda painted shoe boxes of various sizes flat white, and each child made a doll bed, sponge painting the boxes and choosing fabric scraps for blankets and sheets. They put their dolls to bed under their cubbies. "I put him in a bed and put the blanket on," said one boy. Some children created pictures of the dolls in their beds.

The children's interest began to fade naturally once the dolls were put in their beds, and with the program year ending, the teachers began wondering how to put the project itself to bed. They held a party at which the children, families, teachers, and dolls sat together for a celebratory meal, saying good-bye to everyone. The dolls, along with their clothes and beds, went home with the children.

The field trip to the hotel was quite amazing. If we'd been told that a hotel would let children take apart a bed and also jump on it, we no doubt would have been skeptical. Yet that is what happened. From this experience perhaps we can learn not to dismiss good ideas as impossible until we have explored all the options. In terms of the community's understanding of children's thinking, we definitely learned that explanations of children's projects are crucial.

Reflections

Many interconnecting threads were woven during the six-month project. Most critical to its success was the commitment of the teachers. Susan notes that organization was essential in keeping the content going and the interest level up. In weekly planning meetings the teachers brainstormed possibilities, developed questions to ask the children, and thought about probable responses.

It wasn't easy, though. With planning that is responsive rather than programmed, teachers don't know what comes next until they collaborate on devising the best plan to suit the children's responses and interests. This approach can create a climate of uncertainty. Yet uncertainty, like conflict, is a characteristic of professional practice (Schon 1983; 1987).

In previous chapters, we visited the issues around organization and planning, together with the delicate balancing act between being prepared while also being responsive and emergent. One of the reasons this project is such a good example of emergent curriculum is that the teachers, although new to this approach, succeeded in achieving this balance. There was much organization and planning, yes, but not until the children's responses had been heard at each stage. Betty Jones and John Nimmo (1994, 12) refer to the need to "plan and let go," and this project is a good example of just that.

Support for the Project

According to Susan, "A great deal of support is needed outside the classroom because of the time constraints for the teachers. The transcriptions alone took ages." Having someone who could work on the details of organizing documentation processes and assemble the finished panels was essential. The documentation panels consisted of texts of children's conversations, photographs, and drawings. Susan says the panels show to others the path of the curriculum; they make learning visible. The documentation panels completed by managerial staff validated the teachers' work, offering it in visible form to families and other teachers in the center. Although time-consuming to construct, panels are an informative, dramatic, and thought-provoking tool for teacher reflection; they help carry a project forward.

The teachers appreciated the director's implicit support of the project and her appreciation of the results. They also were indebted to the art consultant for her invaluable contribution.

The support of the community buoyed the teachers. When Joelle first proposed the field trip to a hotel to investigate beds, the other teachers' reaction was, "They won't let us come." But the business response was positive, like the hair salon closing for the morning so the children could explore in depth. Joelle's confidence was rewarded, and she now says she is willing to call any place and ask if the children can visit.

Finally, as parents became excited about the project, the teachers were affirmed.

We all know that many teachers do not have time for flexible routines, meetings, or support for creating documentation. Within our programs, we do what we can with the time we have. If your center can provide you with only a half hour per week to yourself, you will need to decide how best to use that time: In dialogue with your team in order to make decisions together? In documenting what has already happened? In making phone calls in order to set up a field trip? If you are interested in project work, there is nothing to be lost—and much to be gained—by asking for support. The answer might be no, or you could find yourself surprised by an alternate scenario. In the last chapter of this book, we will visit a wonderful project that was conducted by a student with no support from her community or from colleagues. She did it alone.

Children's Development

Heather believes the children's drawings showed their development in significant ways. Because the topic was so close to the children's deep interests, "It made their representations really meaningful, both to them and to us." She thinks the emotional involvement fostered much more elaborate representations than are typically seen in this age group. The teachers encouraged these representations by keeping drawing materials at hand and by sitting and chatting with the children as they drew.

According to Bobbi, the children experienced a deep focus by revisiting conversations and activities over and over to peel back further layers of thinking and learning. Carol Anne suggests that a doll for each child created a focal point for making each child's thinking, desires, and experiences visible. This was particularly helpful because two- and three-year-olds are not yet fully verbal.

The children's actions with the dolls and their conversations about them showed teachers what the children noticed and what they desired. In this way the dolls themselves became a form of documentation that the teachers could "read" in deciding what to plan next. Carol Anne thinks the project's power came in part from the children's identification with their dolls, as one identifies with an important character in a book. Such empathy results in deeply meaningful events for children.

Because the interactions with the community were so profound, Joelle sees the outings as the most valuable aspect of the project. "Not only did the children grow, but so did the community: they just opened up to us," she says. The workers at the hair salon, optometrist's office, and hotel were delighted with the visits and expressed surprise at the questions and genuine interest of the two- and three-year-olds. According to the teachers, the people in these work settings saw the children as thinking humans rather than merely cute kids.

The teachers also believe the community considered them more as professionals when they saw them supporting children's interests.

Heather explains, "For the children it's serious: they're investigating the world and we're enhancing that. Going into the community made us look a lot more professional."

For many programs across the United States and Canada, and indeed around the world, tracking development is of huge importance. Teachers seek developmentally appropriate ways of providing assessment of children's development. As teachers within this project reflect on what the children learned, we can see much that could be applied to an assessment or a portfolio—with not a checklist in sight.

Teacher Development

From the perspective of those outside the classroom, as the project progressed month by month the teachers' decision making became more assured, creative, and inspired.

The teachers' images of themselves as teachers altered during the project. Joelle's language use with children changed considerably. She learned to provide a running commentary on children's actions ("You're putting your eyes on the doll's tummy") rather than telling them what to do ("Put the eyes on the face"). She realized that describing back their actions to the children is better for their decision making, and this helped her slow down to observe children's responses more carefully.

Witnessing the children's development in representational skills and interest opened the teachers' eyes to children's potential. And it reinforced Bobbi's belief in arts-based learning. She realized that two- and three-year-olds could understand much more about their bodies than she had thought: "I didn't know that, developmentally, children of two and three could do this," she says. "I thought children in [Reggio Emilia] Italy must be extremely intelligent—they must have pencils in the womb. I didn't know children here could do that."

Heather believes that teachers naturally try to provide children with "the best that you know." But in the press of daily classroom life, she says, teachers worry about "stagnating, not looking for things for yourself as a teacher." Heather adds, "Not that we were doing anything bad [before the project], but we just weren't using our potential." The teachers felt they would do such a project again, because they learned so much from it. Heather thinks she would focus on small-group rather than whole-group involvement. Bobbi thinks she would concentrate on more thought-provoking questions.

As Bobbi says, "The doll project not only permitted us to teach children but also showed parents and the community what children can do. The project put the meaning back in the word teacher."

Edwards, C., L. Gandini, and G. Forman, eds. 1993. *The Hundred Languages of Children: The Reggio Emilia Approach to Early Childhood Education.* Norwood, N.J.: Ablex.

Hendrick, J., ed. 1997. *First Steps toward Teaching the Reggio Way.* Upper Saddle River, N.J.: Prentice Hall.

Schon, D. 1983. *The Reflective Practitioner: How Professionals Think in Action.* New York: Basic Books.

Schon, D. 1987. *Educating the Reflective Practitioner: Towards a New Design for Teaching and Learning in the Professions.* San Francisco, Calif.: Jossey-Bass.

The Child's Voice: A Day in the Life

What is it like for a child to spend his or her days in child care, perhaps from toddlerhood to school age? Do children look forward to their days, or do they crave time at home? Recently, a Halifax director, Susan Willis, expressed her thinking on this topic, telling me, "I often tell teachers that I hope the children wake up in the morning and say 'I wonder what we will do at child care today!' That sense of anticipation, of something new and exciting soon to unfold, is the essence of learning. I would want my staff to feel that way too."

A day in a classroom where emergent curriculum is in use has the potential to feel comfortable to the child, in that the very structure and routines within the day, as well as the program and physical environment, are created with the child's thinking in mind—not

"How we are going to move the children through the day?" but "How should this day evolve so that we respect the child's rhythms, interests, and capabilities?" Let's imagine a day that is constructed in this way.

Sam enters the preschool room with Dad at 8 A.M., after having eaten his breakfast muffin in the car on the way to school. Although he's been attending this child care setting for about three months, he still has a hard time letting Dad leave each morning. A teacher comes over to the door to greet them. Another teacher is working with a small group of children in the block area, Sam's favorite place to be.

Dad can stay with Sam for a few minutes this morning, so they sit in the armchair close to the door. While Sam scribbles his own name on the children's attendance list, Dad takes a quick look at the documentation panel that is at eye level from his seated position. They spot Sam in one of the photos, and talk about the project and what Sam was doing. Another parent and child enter, and at this point it's time for Sam's dad to leave. While she greets the new arrivals, the teacher also takes Sam's hand and tells him, "There's something special in the block area today!" Dad gives Sam a quick hug and leaves. Sam's lower lip begins to tremble, and the teacher crouches down to hug him while she chats with the arriving parents. She holds onto Sam until he's ready to let go, and then escorts both children to the block area.

Sam is surprised to see short tree trunks in the block area. Yesterday, he and his two best buddies had an idea about tree houses. Sam had told his friend that kids could build real tree houses, he'd seen it on TV, but his friends said kids couldn't do that because they were too high and you had to use dangerous tools. Now, as Sam sits and runs his hands over the logs, the second teacher, Pam, asks, "Remember your idea about tree houses?" Sam nods. "Well," continues Pam, "I wonder if there's a way to join these logs together so you can show your friends what you meant . . ."

Sam and his friends spend the next hour experimenting with the logs. As needed, Pam provides small pulleys, bungee cords, and string. She refers the children to the woodworking area when they decide they need some small planks. As more and more children arrive, so does another teacher, and the classroom now is in full swing. Playtime lasts two hours, and Sam is not interrupted to join snack. His friends go to eat and then come back, but Sam stops only for juice and then continues building.

When he notices Pam writing, he asks what she's writing about. "I'm writing about what you're doing," she says, and then gets the digital camera. She shows the three builders the photos she's taken, and, after looking at them, they decide their tree house needs to be "taller than us" and so continue building. Sometimes Sam is distracted by other activities in areas of the room and goes to take a look. Pam protects the complex building while he's away. Soon, the lead teacher goes around the room and says to each group of children, "We have about ten more minutes before circle time!" As an aside to Pam, she adds, "We can let it go longer if they are still deeply into this."

At 10 A.M., a full two hours after Sam arrived, many children are ready to clean up and come to circle. Sam is happy to join circle, but not to clean up. He and his friends are very proud of their tree house. Pam tells the boys to leave their structure right there, and the lead teacher gathers the circle around the perimeter of the block building surrounding it.

The children go through their familiar greetings and songs, and then Pam asks Sam and his two friends to explain the building they've been working on. Sam gets up and walks around while pointing to various aspects of the structure. The other children have lots of questions. One of them asks "Are you leaving it there forever?"

The group brainstorms all the possible ways they could save the building: through photos, through drawings, or by putting a label on it saying "Do not knock down." Everyone agrees that it takes up a lot of space, so no one else could play in that area. Then one of the five-year-olds says, "We should really build it outside, around the big old tree," and the three builders think this is a great idea. The block structure is left standing for the time being.

After circle, the children disperse into small groups. Sam is in a group that's been learning to use clay. Lena, his small-group teacher, asks him, "Do you think you could show me your tree house using clay?" Sam is eager to try. He has a hard time joining all the pieces together, but Lena helps him to score and wet the clay edges to make them stick. Another child finds twigs on the art shelf and brings them over for Sam to use. His model is put on a shelf to dry, and the children head outside one by one as they finish.

After much rough and tumble play, Sam pauses by the tree. He tells Pam, "It's too tall for me to make a tree house up there," and she takes photos of the tree for the children to think about during circle the following day.

When the children come in from outdoor play, their lunch boxes sit at the tables for them to open. Except for a boy with severe allergies who must sit next to a teacher, everyone chooses their own seat. Noisy chatter continues throughout lunch. As one by one the children finish eating, they put their lunch boxes away and head for the bathroom area. When children start moving away from the tables, Pam sets out rest mats, and some of the children help her, for they all know where the mats belong. It's Jane's turn to choose the CD, and soon, as the children return from the bathroom and lie down, the soft sound of wind and birds fills the room. Lights are dimmed.

Sam, who doesn't sleep during the day at home and has no rest times there, is restless. He doesn't understand why he has to lie down at school, and he tells this to Lena. "I know," she replies, "but here at school we have to relax for just a little bit. You don't have to sleep. Why don't you just listen to the music, and I'll get you a book." She returns with a couple of favorites, and Sam looks at them for nearly forty-five minutes before asking to get up.

After Lena helps him fold his mat and put it away, Sam notices small tables set up with activities. He plays alone at one of them and then with two other early wakers. He chats with all three teachers as they come and go from their lunch breaks. This is Sam's favorite time. It's quiet, and he can do lots of different things without having to be with all the kids. He likes school better when it's peaceful. Once all the children are awake, they have snack, and this time Sam chooses to join them.

Then they have choices to make. It's raining out, so they can choose to go to the multipurpose room for music and movement—which Sam likes a lot—or to the infant room if they have a brother or sister there—which Sam does not—or go for a walk in the rain to the mailroom on campus to pick up the school's mail. Sam chooses the walk.

Along with three or four other children, Sam spends the next half hour getting dressed in rain gear, splashing in puddles while walking outside, and then delivering mail to the director, the administrative assistant, and the teachers. He feels important, and he decides it would be a good idea to be a mail carrier when he grows up. He tells this to Pam, and she asks him why. "Because you get to go outside in the rain, and carry a big pouch," he tells her. Pam writes this down.

When they get back to the classroom, Pam invites Sam to go to the writing area and draw a mail carrier. He decides instead to draw the big pouch with letters peeking out of the top. As he works at writing *Mail* under his drawing, Pam scaffolds by encouraging him to think about the beginning letter sound. From there, he uses invented spelling. She helps him put the drawing and her note into his folder.

There's still time for more play after all the children have returned from around the school. Pam gathers Sam and his building friends and they discuss what to do with their big building, which is still standing. They decide they'll take more pictures to show their parents, put away the blocks, and make a plan to take some materials outside tomorrow, when they'll build again. Pam, who writes a note to herself and one in the teachers' log on the counter, knows that she'll be looking for books on tree houses tonight.

The day begins to wind down. Sam knows his mom will be picking him up tonight, and he's standing on a low bench near a window from which the children can watch the parking lot as parents arrive. Spotting his mom's car, he makes a beeline for the door. When she comes in, he first jumps into her arms and then pulls her over to the photos on the table in the parent area. She sits in the comfy armchair and tells him, "Quick, show me! We have to go home for supper, and Dad has a meeting to get to tonight." Sam explains the photos, and they prepare to leave as Lena comes over to say good-night. She has only a few seconds to connect with Mom, but they laugh together, and Sam feels good. He asks, "Is Lena your friend?" and Mom says, "Yes! We're getting to know each other pretty well."

On their way through the lobby, Sam selects one of the little packages of animal crackers set out in a basket for children to take as they leave. They're often hungry on the drive home. In the car, Mom asks, "How was your day? What did you do?" "Oh," Sam replies, "I just played."

For Sam this day seemed quite uneventful. But early childhood educators can see that the teachers addressed Sam's emotional needs; supported his interests; were able to scaffold his learning about tree houses, building, and literacy; documented his work; provided opportunities for new experiences and connection with the campus community; provided for both quiet and energetic activities; and worked on building a relationship with Sam. On Sam's part, the structure of the day also provided for decision making, negotiating, making choices, and resting. Thus, this simple day was complete from both Sam's and the teachers' perspectives.

Suggested Reading

Fraser, S., and C. Gestwicki. 2002. *Authentic Childhood: Exploring Reggio Emilia in the Classroom*. Albany, N.Y.: Delmar.

9
Emergent Curriculum as a Creative Act

Imagine being so deeply engaged in both the interactive and intellectual sides of your teaching work that the bland routines of the day seem less pressing. You look forward to both problem finding and problem solving and finding stimulating challenges in daily events as they unfold. You meet such a day with eager anticipation, a feeling of "Let's get going!" or "I wonder." People in other lines of work might have to face boredom each day, but early childhood educators are rarely bored. While respecting the professional guidelines and boundaries of our field, we have the opportunity to be original and creative in our work, to be open to the unexpected.

Think about a time when you were so deeply engaged in an activity, or a hobby, or some intriguing problem that time and your surroundings simply fell away. Can you remember being in your own world, relaxed and yet focused at the same time? Perhaps this happened more often when you were a child and completely absorbed with friends in acting out some complex scenario while trying to solve a problem: How can we make a roof for the tree house with just these things we've found? How will we join it all together? And how will we get up there?

You might recognize this feeling of absorption if you are involved with the arts or with making things, or if you enjoy the challenges of complex puzzles, crosswords,

159

or mind-bending games. Although these activities pose challenges for us, they are also fun. They engage both the left and right sides of our brain, requiring that we immerse ourselves in the challenge and think creatively, and lead us to a feeling of what Mihaly Csikszentmihaly calls "flow" (Csikszentmihaly 1996, 110).

Throughout this book, we have talked about responsiveness, the idea of generating curriculum from emerging interests rather than from following prescribed curricula—in other words, harnessing creativity. Even if you don't think of yourself as a creative person, emergent curriculum provides an environment where original responses to children are possible. With emergent curriculum, your creativity is facilitated by the children. Given the opportunity, the time, and the materials, children are original in their thinking, in their play ideas, and in their solutions to challenges. When we think deeply about what they are doing, their ideas have the capability of provoking novel responses from us.

As we watch children within the classroom, we are constantly gathering information. Sometimes we do this consciously—as in writing down observations or taking photographs. Sometimes we store in our subconscious the input from what is going on all around us and it isn't revealed until we reflect on the day or the week with other teachers. A wonderful thing happens when we share all this information; we begin to see things from many perspectives and think of new ways to approach the work. The potential for creativity is there.

When we teachers bring our professional expertise, judgment, prior knowledge, and experience to the creative process, we are able to trust our judgment and feel secure in the decisions we make. And this remains true even when the resulting curriculum decisions are out of the ordinary compared to traditional early childhood curricula developed by others.

Using Creativity for Curriculum

The two sides of our brain have different functions. Whereas the left side processes verbal information and treats information in analytical and sequential ways, the right side focuses on visual/spatial information and processes information in a more intuitive, divergent, and simultaneous manner.

To be more creative in our thinking, we need to exercise our right brain. In the industrialized world, however, left-brained thinking has become dominant. We live by our routines, supported by technology and timetables, planners and schedules. Can we break away from this stance, even for just enough time to generate open and creative responses to young children? Some early childhood instructors, programs, and teachers regularly use brainstorming and creative activity in their meetings to facilitate a higher degree of creativity.

Whether your school or center uses one type of meeting for business/organizational matters and another for curriculum discussions, or instead combines the two, it is useful to realize that these two agendas require completely different mind-sets. If the meetings you attend combine both agendas, it may be worth working on gaining access to the creative part of your brain before trying to generate new or provocative approaches to teaching. You can do this in several ways, and it can be playful and open ended.

Using Novel Materials

If we expect children to freely explore new materials, we teachers must experience the same sense of discovery and perhaps disequilibrium that children experience, so that we fully understand how an experience may feel for them. Have you, for instance, explored watercolor, clay, and wire to represent your ideas? Have you figured out how to use pulleys effectively, or how to measure a flower without a tape measure?

Before a staff meeting at CFDC, teachers were asked to experience smooth rocks on their own, in silence, for several minutes. As they became engaged in the activity, some experienced the purely sensory aspect of the rocks, while others focused on the rocks' intricate designs. After several minutes, a sense of relaxation and calm surmounted the busy workday. Tabletop mirrors were then offered to each person as an invitation, and these were used in novel ways with the rocks. Following this exercise, we discussed the children's use of classroom materials. Brainstorming for future directions stemmed from this relaxed yet stimulated mind-set.

Beginning with Dialogue: A Warm-up for Curriculum Discussions

For early childhood educators, meetings are always restricted by time. Even so, you may find that meetings are both more productive and more creative if you begin with sharing rather than planning. A free-flowing conversation, even for a few minutes, can help us to loosen up a little. A lead teacher, the director, or some other provocateur might ask something such as "What puzzled you this week?" or "What challenged your thinking today?" This kind of sharing ultimately leads to discussion of observations and is less constricting than asking a question like "What are we going to do tomorrow?"

Using the Expertise of Those Outside Our Field

What captures your attention when you walk past a store window? When you flip idly through a decorating magazine? When you meander through an art gallery? Being mindful of the work of those outside our own field—for instance, those in the graphic arts, merchandising and display, and interior design—can lead to creative ways of approaching our own work on documentation, classroom environments, and the use of materials outside of the usual early childhood sources. In a curriculum meeting, you might want to share an unexpected material or source, a different way of displaying children's work, a photograph or an example of graphic design that stirs your imagination. Remember, too, that creative professionals from outside our field can be friends of early childhood. By inviting them to engage with children younger than they are perhaps used to, learning opportunity arises for all the involved parties—visitors, children, and teachers alike.

Sharing Inspiration from Writers in Other Fields

If your team members are avid readers of early childhood publications, beginning a meeting with inspirations from their reading can be valuable. But let's not neglect the words of other writers. For instance, Dorothea Brande, in *Becoming a Writer*, talks about recapturing "innocence of eye." She says, "Refuse to allow yourself to go about wrapped in a cloak of oblivion. . . . For half an hour each day transport yourself back to the state of wide-eyed interest that was yours at the age of five" (Brande 1961, 114). Although Brande's context is the creative writing process, her words speak to early childhood educators and can be shared as a source of inspiration.

Invitations: Toward Creativity

An invitation, of course, can be either accepted or declined. You may or may not choose to take up the following suggestions in your journey toward a more emergent approach to teaching. At the very least, they may add interest to your classroom or routine. In the best-case scenario, they offer a chance to work toward a responsive and rewarding curriculum for both you and the children.

Cultivate Curiosity

We learn best what we are curious about. We may well understand this in terms of children's learning, but we must remember that it's equally true of adults. Retain your curiosity. Wonder about children, and with them. For example, I recently watched children construct Santa's sleigh from chairs and shelves (with toys piled on top, of course!) and then proceed to tie themselves to it with scarves from the dancing area, and prance like reindeer, with their arms bent in front, as they leapt about. As I watched this most unusual prancing motion, I wondered, "How do they know how to do that? From a film, a song, a book? I wonder what 'prancing' means to them. How do children understand the movements of different animals?"

As you watch children, allow yourself to formulate questions about what is going on.

Be a Stranger in Your Own Classroom

When you are alone in your classroom at the beginning or the end of the day, try to see this environment from the perspective of someone who has never been there before. What feeling does the classroom evoke? You may find that this can vary from comfort to unease, from delight to confusion, from security to curiosity. Think about both your response and what a child's response might be in entering the classroom as a newcomer. How does the classroom speak to you? If you have trouble seeing your classroom through new eyes, try photographs of your environment and examine them as a new way to see your space.

Treat Your Classroom Environment as a Piece of Documentation

What do the walls, activities, materials, and artwork in your classroom say about your philosophy and the children's work? What about the furnishings themselves and how they are arranged? How independent can the children be in this environment? How is the children's thinking made explicit? How is your voice as the teacher represented? You can make all of these components explicit in the form of documentation, which can then be understood by others as they examine the classroom.

Shape Your Space and Challenge Your Own Assumptions

Sometimes when we think about trying new things in our workplace, an internal voice says, "That wouldn't be allowed," or "We have to do it the way we're doing it right now." If you'd like to try new approaches and refresh your work, I encourage you to ignore that voice and simply discuss your ideas with your supervisor, or your team, or the whole center, if staff meetings allow for this kind of discussion. There is everything to be gained by taking a few small steps in a new direction, and the first step can be to simply talk about ideas.

Erect Barriers to Protect Your Time to Think

As educators, we are forever attempting to break down barriers. We want classrooms that respect diversity, colleagues with whom we can easily communicate, and an open relationship with our supervisors. There is one barrier, however, that I suggest you maintain. You need to protect your time for reflection. Carving out time for thinking is difficult, but it's essential. If this means you must get away at lunchtime to a place where you can find solitude, you need to weigh that against the need for collegiality in the staff room and find a balance. If you find it easier to reflect during dialogue with others, you will need to conspire to make that a priority for your team. If your drive home is when you think about the day, you won't want to be listening to endless traffic reports or news on the radio. Protect your thinking space—it's difficult to find, and you must guard it.

Seek a Balance between Creativity and Organization

Emergent curriculum requires both creativity and organization, which work together, not in opposition. To be a reflective and creative teacher, you also need to organize your time and space. You want materials at hand when you need them so you can be responsive to both your own questions and the children's ideas. Finally, time spent in organizing your space will pay off when something serendipitous arises.

Recognize What You Really Enjoy

If we are honest with ourselves, we know what we are good at. A feeling of "rightness" arises when we make a good decision, and children certainly let us know if we're off track! We can capitalize on our strengths, especially when we work in a team. If, for instance, you are a terrific observer and notetaker, you can assume a leadership role in this aspect of emergent curriculum, modeling for others, sharing your observations, and encouraging others to observe. If another team member has an eye for stunning documentation, the whole team will benefit, and everyone can offer verbal input as the documentation develops. Discuss your strengths as a team, support and encourage each other, and be sure to let your colleagues know when they have inspired you.

Develop an Open Mind

Teamwork requires taking on others' perspectives, and that calls for practice. Rather than avoiding discussion of differing opinions, listen carefully and be open to what others are seeing and thinking. When you hear three different interpretations of one observation—and this does happen—it's possible to formulate three different responses, in the form of classroom invitations. No one has to be right and everyone has a voice. The children's responses will tell you which direction you should pursue further.

The Teacher's Voice: The Laundry Day Project

In the previous chapter, we examined the Doll Project, which was supported by several people, with teachers constantly collaborating in making decisions. The result was a very creative project that was unusual in its depth. But what if you work completely alone, with no administrator, no colleagues, and little opportunity to meet with other educators? Under those circumstances, is it possible to be creative in response to the children?

Shelly Donnelly is an experienced family child care provider in rural New Hampshire. She has converted an annex of her home into a warm and welcoming child care space, and her facility is a licensed family setting for up to six children. Shelly has been working with young children ranging in age from infancy to kindergarten for eight years while attending school part-time to earn her associate degree in early childhood education. Shelly thus represents many early childhood educators in North America—she has her own family, she runs a full time child care program, and she goes to school in the evenings. Despite this incredibly busy lifestyle and many demands on her time, Shelly is a thoughtful practitioner who is truly committed to early childhood education and who strives to grow.

As a member of my practicum class, Shelly was required to carry out an emergent curriculum project during the winter semester. For this assignment, students were to use their observations to guide their decision making and also document the whole process—including their own reflections on what happened. Given the nature of emergent curriculum, students could carry out this assignment on a time line dictated by the children. Whenever the opportunity arose during the semester, students would begin their assignment, and when the children moved on to other interests or tangents, student teachers could complete their documentation and submit the assignment. In this way, time lines and length of projects were very flexible.

In practicum seminars, Shelly was often perplexed, and she shared her frustrations with us. She explained that her children ranged from one year to five years old, that she worked alone, and that the children were often "all over the place" with their play and interests. Shelly offered an example: at one point there were two preschool children playing at pirates, another who had recently experienced the addition of a new sibling to the family, and an infant who of course was fascinated with watching the older children at play. How could she find a thread to follow? We often discussed the fact that an emerging project needn't involve all children, but since she was working alone, this didn't help Shelly. No matter what topic she chose to pursue, the infant still needed careful attention and she had to make lunch and do other practical chores while at the same time addressing the wide developmental needs of the group. Shelly often set out invitations—sometimes around the pirate play she'd observed—but didn't feel that the children fully engaged with them. She was truly stuck.

Meanwhile, the day-to-day life of her program continued. As is true with many family providers, Shelly's practical chores often interrupted her teaching role. It was one of these practical chores—doing the laundry—that provided the solution to Shelly's puzzle. First one child and then two led Shelly into this short yet extremely meaningful project. But let's look at Shelly's project in its entirety and hear the story in her own words. We begin with her first observations.

April 11

After nap I watched as Brodyn struggled to fold his own blanket to put it away. Seeing this, I wondered, "Why not just show all the children how to fold a blanket?" Kyle was a bit hesitant, but he spread out his blanket and I showed him how to fold these two corners to those two corners, turn it and do it again. I commented, "See—it's getting smaller—it's almost done." When he finished, Kyle said, "I did it, Shelly! Look at that—cool."

April 12

While I was putting a load of laundry into my washer, Brodyn came over and asked, "Do you need any help with that?" I told him "Sure!" and he started putting a white shirt in the washer. But I was washing darks, so I explained to him, "I only want really dark clothes for this load—can you find the really dark clothes in the basket?" "Why?" he asked. I explained, "If I wash white or really light clothes with the dark clothes, sometimes the color in the dark clothes swishes around in the water and sticks to the light clothes and makes them look dirty instead of clean." "Oh," he said, "Is this one okay?" as he picked up a dark blue T-shirt. I told him, "Perfect." Kyle joined us and asked, "Can I help too?" I answered, "Sure, Kyle, I'll tell you what, Brodyn can find the dark clothes and you can put them in the washer for me." The boys were able to successfully sort and load the laundry together.

April 13

After I changed the dramatic play space into a laundry room, Kyle and Brodyn showed a new interest in the space. Brodyn began "washing" the baby blankets and towels and then ironing and folding them. After folding a few, he realized he'd forgotten to dry them, so he asked me what you do first, wash or iron. I gave him a brief explanation and he said, "Oh great, now I have to take all these out and start over!" He put the clothes in the washer, held up the detergent and fabric softener bottles, and asked, "Which one do I put in here?" I explained that the dark blue bottle was the laundry soap that cleans the clothes like soap cleans our hands, and the light blue bottle was fabric softener that makes the clothes feel soft and smell good.

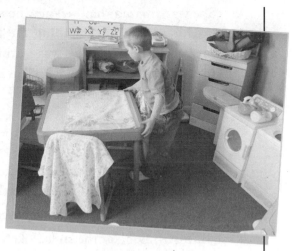

When Kyle comes into the housekeeping area, Brodyn says, "Kyle, want to help me? Can you get all the baby clothes so I can wash them?" Seeming uninterested, Kyle says "Noooo," so Brodyn suggests, "I'll get the clothes and you can spin the washer if you want." Kyle says no again and Brodyn continues his play alone. After the wash is done, Brodyn puts the clothes in the dryer and asks me, "Now do I have to put this one [fabric softener] in here [the dryer]?" I explained again that the fabric softener is added in the washer. He starts taking all the clothes out of the dryer and putting them back in the washer to rewash them. When the clothes are washed again and then dried, Brodyn begins to iron them. He stops and says, "Shelly, I think I did it wrong. I forgot I have to iron before I dry these." I explained that clothes have to be cleaned, then dried, then ironed. After ironing a receiving blanket, he spreads it out on the table to fold it and put it away in the drawer.

April 18

After giving the parents their newsletters earlier this week I received feedback about the laundry piece. Kyle's mother informed me that Kyle has been showing interest in helping her do the laundry, and even knew how to fold the towels.

She was amazed that he knew how to do that and said she didn't remember ever teaching him. After reading the newsletter, it all made sense to her. She was thrilled to hear that he was learning about such a simple, everyday event, and that he was retaining it as well as enjoying it.

April 19: Field Trip to a Laundromat

We didn't actually wash clothes while at the laundromat—we observed others going through the laundry process. The people doing laundry were very cooperative and just loved to see that I was teaching the children about laundry.

We followed through the process, beginning with the washer.

BRODYN: Look at the suds. Like when we wash our hands—soap gets them clean, right?

SHELLY: Right, and do you know how you get the soap off your hands?

KYLE: Water!

SHELLY: Yes, and after the washer is done swishing the soap bubbles all around on the clothes, it will drain the soapy water and add clean water and swish the water all around to wash the bubbles away. Then it drains out all the water by spinning really fast, and then the clothes are ready for the dryer.

SHELLY: The washing part takes awhile, so we can sit down and wait for the washing machine to finish washing the clothes. [We sit and wait and talk while the clothes wash. Finally, the washer stops.]

SHELLY: Okay, the clothes are done washing. What do we have to do next?

BRODYN: Dry them!

KYLE: [repeating right after Brodyn]—Dry them! [We go over to the dryer area and look at how dryers work.]

KYLE: [going over to feel the glass on the dryer] Wow, that's too hot! I don't want to touch it.

BRODYN: Why is it so hot?

SHELLY: Let's see if the washing machine was hot.

BRODYN: [running over and feeling it] Nope, it's cold.

SHELLY: Clothes dry faster when they get warm air blown on them. So who remembers what we do with the clothes after we dry them?

BRODYN: You fold them on the bed.

SHELLY: Yes, sometimes clothes get folded on the bed, but at a laundromat there are no beds, so we fold them on a big table. [We watch a person fold clothes for a minute.]

SHELLY: Do you think that's the last part of doing the laundry?

BRODYN: Nooooo, you have to put them in your van.

SHELLY: Right, but then what do you do with the laundry?

BRODYN: You bring it in your house, right?

SHELLY: Yes . . . Do you leave them in the laundry basket when you get them home?

KYLE: Nooooo.

SHELLY: What do you think you do with them, Kyle?

KYLE: Um, I forget.

SHELLY: Brodyn, do you remember?

BRODYN: I think you have to put them away.

SHELLY: [singing part of the laundry song she previously invented and shared with the children] So they're ready to . . .

BRODYN: [singing] Wear another day.

April 19

When we got home I showed the children how the water was spun out, and we made a list of all the words we learned.

To help the children understand how the water is spun out of the clothes, we did an experiment using wet doll clothes and a salad spinner to spin out the water. Brodyn said, "Look at the water that we spun out!"

April 20

Not surprisingly, I didn't succeed in finding a book that taught children the steps of doing the laundry. The children thought we should make a book. To involve them in creating the book, I asked them to draw pictures of all the stages of doing laundry. I decided to take photos from our laundromat field trip and add them to the pages along with the pictures the children created. It was a lot of work, but it

was worth it in the end. Each child has a copy and knows that they were part of this.

Using pictures of Brodyn doing the laundry steps in the housekeeping area, I was able to make sequence cards for the children to use in practicing the steps.

To represent the steps of doing laundry, we also made a cycle chart to hang in the classroom. The parents were then able to see the children helping me do a load of laundry at my house. We turned the steps into a song. As I taught them the song I made up, I had them fill in certain words. Creating both a song and a panel using the words made it easier for them to remember the words by looking at the pictures, and easier to follow the cycle by singing the song. A perfect combination.

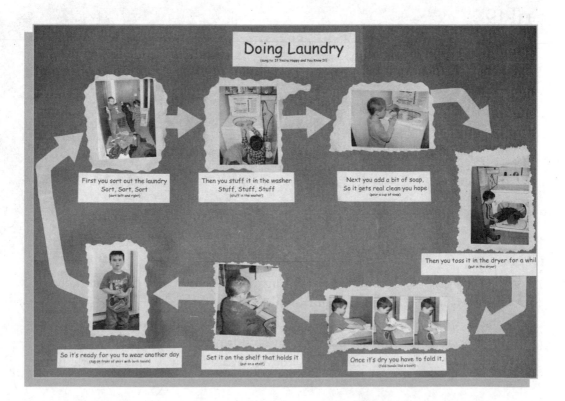

Reflection on the Laundry Day Project

During your first visit to my child care, you made the comment that I didn't really need curriculum books in order to develop activities and projects. But I asked myself, how can I possibly come up with ideas for scaffolding every topic that children are interested in? I didn't really understand emergent curriculum at that time.

My initial choice was a project about babies, since two of the children in my care were going to be big brothers this year and they spent a lot of time playing with the dolls and in the role of mom or dad. Then another child began playing pirates, so I wanted to focus on that topic. But he ended up leaving my program, and the other children never talked about pirates again. So I kept my eyes open for the perfect focus. Suddenly, there it was, right in front of my eyes. Something as simple as teaching the children how to do laundry became the perfect emergent curriculum project.

I have to admit that, falling back on old habits, I tried to find ready-to-use ideas to use for this project, but all I could find was ideas for sorting and counting laundry. I wanted the children to understand the entire process, since they were so curious about that. Every idea in this project came from me and the children brainstorming, or from me having to find ways to answer their questions (for example, the salad spinner activity). We made clip-art sequence cards from scratch. Every part of this project was satisfying. I never opened a curriculum book for ideas, yet the children's questions were answered and they constructed lots of knowledge that built on their curiosity.

When I went to do a presentation on family child care to other students in the Foundations classes, they asked what type of activities I do and I told them about this most recent work with the children. The professors were surprised to hear of such a project. They'd never thought of working with children on this kind of practical knowledge. To me, that is one of the wonderful aspects of having a home child care setting. Why not teach children about groceries, gardening, sweeping, laundry, or clearing the table after dinner? Maria Montessori did it, and so can we. I believe that it's very useful in terms of the children's future, since these are the tools they will use as adults, and they are naturally fascinated with them. (One of my child care parents told me that when she was in college she had two roommates who had no idea how to make their beds or do laundry!) We can't overlook the opportunity to teach our children these everyday practicalities of life.

Emergent curriculum is such a powerful teaching process. I have learned that teaching shouldn't be from a plan book of prescribed activities—it should be from the child's mind.

Reflecting on Shelly's Work

When we consider that this was the first emergent project Shelly had ever attempted, it's exciting to see that it is so complete. Shelly paid attention to an everyday conversation that demonstrated a child's curiosity about laundry. Such conversations, I suspect, happen several times a day in child care settings, no matter whether they're based in centers or homes. Children, after all, are naturally curious about adult tasks. Using a few observations as a starting point, Shelly adapted the environment by changing the dramatic play area. She documented what happened during this invitation, and noticed a child struggling with the sequencing. Then we see some scaffolding taking place. The children needed more real-life experience, so their teacher took them to another place where laundry is done—the laundromat. Not a usual choice for a field trip, yet an inspired one. Here, the children could see the big picture of how everyone does laundry. And again, Shelly documented with photography and a transcription of the children's questions and her explanations.

Back at the center, Shelly had a very original idea to help children understand the spinning that expels water from the clothing. She gave them a salad spinner to explore using wet doll clothing. She then incorporated a literacy component that helped the children understand the laundry process—they made a book together. And, still wanting to do something about that sequencing struggle, Shelly made cards for the children to put into order (a key experience in seriation). And, in the middle of all this, Shelly managed to send home a parent newsletter that included an explanation of what was going on within the project, thereby making clear to parents why their children suddenly knew how to fold towels!

What we see through studying this documentation is a very complete process. This teacher noticed an interest, jotted down some brief notes about it, changed the environment to invite dramatic play, and watched again. Then she took the children out into the wider community, followed up with additional activities that scaffolded further understanding, documented all of this, communicated with parents, and then reflected on the whole process.

Thinking about Shelly's attention to real-life work and her thoughtful scaffolding, we might be reminded of connections to Dewey, Montessori, and Vygotsky. Thus, this example of generating emergent curriculum brings home the point that we don't necessarily need activity books, prescribed curriculum, or resources generated by others. What we need is focused attention on the children.

Teachers Have the Last Word

The educators in this book have been generous in sharing their stories, their struggles, and their approaches. In the form of further invitations, they offer you just a few more words:

> Ask yourself these questions: What in your environment delights children and makes them question? What do children do with these materials/provocations that make *you* question? How can you explore this?
>
> Doing anything new can be overwhelming. Consider where your passion lies. What have you wondered about with your practice? Could this be a good place to begin?
>
> Liz Hicks, early childhood consultant, Halifax, Nova Scotia

> Think of the possibilities for curriculum in the same way that we hope children will when we give them open-ended toys. Trust the process—when you do, there is always something to learn from it rather than only to be pleased or disappointed in the results.
>
> Teresa Cosgrove, college instructor, Port William, Oregon

> Make a habit of documenting ordinary moments. I like to think of these daily observations as beads. Beading is something that I enjoy in my personal life. I am always collecting simple, yet interesting beads. I never quite anticipate how they will fit into my next project, so I place them in a box as potential for later use. Likewise, the meaning of the daily notes, or conversations, or pictures I take in the classroom only becomes evident when I discover the larger context that the children create over time. It is then that I start to string the beads together and a project takes form.
>
> Susan Hagner, director, Emerson Preschool, Concord, New Hampshire

Whether you're happy to continue with your present curriculum approach or want to investigate new ways of thinking about curriculum, emergent curriculum offers you a chance to explore wonderful ideas—both the children's and your own. It allows you to be passionate about your work while meeting the professional requirements of our field. You can continue to grow as an educator if you take your wonderful ideas and then work hard by thinking with others, exploring possibilities, and sharing the results with the larger community.

To be able to make educational gold out of emerging activities in the classroom requires a high degree of artistry in teaching.

Elliot W. Eisner, *The Arts and the Creation of Mind*

We work in a challenging field. Let's bring all our expertise and training, as well as our deep sense of responsibility to children, and combine these with playfulness and creativity in order to be open and responsive. When we combine our teaching skills with reflective practices we can become immersed in, and nourished by, the art of emergent curriculum.

Suggested Readings

Csikszentmihaly, M. 1996. *Creativity: Flow and the Psychology of Discovery and Invention.* New York: HarperCollins.

Eisner, E. W. 2002. *The Arts and the Creation of Mind.* New Haven: Yale University Press.

References

Bredekamp, S., and C. Copple, eds. 1997. *Developmentally Appropriate Practices in Early Childhood Programs,* rev. ed. Washington, D.C.: NAEYC

Brande, D. 1961. *Becoming a Writer.* Los Angeles: J. P. Tarcher.

Copley, J., National Association for the Education of Young Children, National Council of Teachers of Mathematics. 2000. *The Young Child and Mathematics.* Washington, D.C.: NAEYC.

Csikszentmihaly, M. 1996. *Creativity: Flow and the Psychology of Discovery and Invention.* New York: HarperCollins.

Curtis, D., and M. Carter. 2000. *The Art of Awareness: How Observation Can Transform Your Teaching.* St. Paul: Redleaf Press.

———— 2003. *Designs for Living and Learning: Transforming Early Childhood Environments.* St. Paul: Redleaf Press.

Edwards, C., L. Gandini, and G. Forman, eds. 1993. *The Hundred Languages of Children: The Reggio Emilia Approach–Advanced Reflections.* 2nd ed. Greenwich, Conn.: Ablex.

Eisner, E. W. 2002. *The Arts and the Creation of Mind.* New Haven: Yale University Press.

Fanelli, S. 1995. *My Map Book.* New York: HarperCollins.

Forman, G. 1996. *Jed Draws His Bicycle: A Case Study of Drawing to Learn* (videotape) Amherst, Mass.: Performanetics.

———— 2000. *Ordinary Moments: Where the Children Live.* Presentation to the Organization Mondial pour L'Education Prescolaire, 5th International Conference on Early Childhood.

Fraser, S., and C. Gestwicki. 2002. *Authentic Childhood: Experiencing Reggio Emilia in the Classroom.* Albany, N.Y.: Delmar Publishing.

Hill, L. T., A. J. Stremmel, and V. R. Fu. 2005. *Teaching as Inquiry: Rethinking Curriculum in Early Childhood Education.* Boston: Pearson Education.

Hohmann, M., and D. P. Weikart. 1995. *Educating Young Children: Active Learning Practices for Preschool and Child Care Programs.* Ypsilanti, Mich.: High/Scope Press.

Jones, E., and J. Nimmo. 1994. *Emergent Curriculum.* Washington, D.C.: NAEYC.

Jones, E., and G. Reynolds. 1992. *The Play's the Thing: Teachers' Roles in Children's Play.* New York: Teachers College Press.

Nicholson, S. 1971. How Not to Cheat Children: The Theory of Loose Parts. *Landscape Architecture* 62(1): 30–34.

Rinaldi, C. 2006. *In Dialogue with Reggio Emilia: Listening, Researching and Learning.* New York: Routledge.

Stacey, S. 2005. Emergent Curriculum: Struggles, Supports, and Successes. Master's thesis, Pacific Oaks College, Calif.

Wien, C. A. 1995. *Developmentally Appropriate Practice in "Real Life": Stories of Teacher Practical Knowledge.* New York: Teachers College Press.

Wien, C. A., and S. Kirby-Smith. 1998. Untiming the Curriculum: A Case Study of Removing Clocks from the Program. *Young Children* 53(5): 8–13.

Wien, C. A., S. Stacey, B.-L. H. Keating, J. D. Rowlings, and H. Cameron. 2002. The Doll Project: Handmade Dolls as a Framework for Emergent Curriculum. *Young Children* 57(1): 33–38.